CHRIS CHRISMAN
GOES TO
COLLEGE

. . . and faces the challenges of
relativism, individualism and pluralism

JAMES W. SIRE

INTERVARSITY PRESS
DOWNERS GROVE, ILLINOIS 60515

InterVarsity Press® is the book-publishing division of InterVarsity Christian Fellowship®, a student movement active on campus at hundreds of universities, colleges and schools of nursing in the United States of America, and a member movement of the International Fellowship of Evangelical Students. For information about local and regional activities, write Public Relations Dept., InterVarsity Christian Fellowship, 6400 Schroeder Rd., P.O. Box 7895, Madison, WI 53707-7895.

Poetry from "Creed" by Steve Turner is taken from Up to Date, copyright 1982 by Steve Turner. Published by Lion Publishing and Hodder and Stoughton Limited. All rights reserved. Used by permission.

All Scripture quotations, unless otherwise indicated, are taken from the HOLY BIBLE, NEW INTERNATIONAL VERSION. Copyright © 1973, 1978, 1984 International Bible Society. Used by permission of Zondervan Publishing House. All rights reserved.

Cover illustration: Kurt Mitchell

ISBN 0-8308-1656-9

Printed in the United States of America ∞

Library of Congress Cataloging-in-Publication Data
Sire, James W.
    Chris Chrisman goes to college—and faces the challenges of
relativism, individualism, and pluralism/James W. Sire.
        p.   cm.
    ISBN 0-8308-1656-9 (alk. paper)
    1. College students—United States—Fiction.   I. Title.
PS3569.I65C47   1993
813'.54—dc20   93-17816
                                                                         CIP

15   14   13   12   11   10   9   8   7   6   5   4   3   2   1
04   03   02   01   00   99   98   97   96   95   94   93

To
Chris Chrisman, Bob Wong, Susie Sylvan, Bill Seipel
and all the students they represent
at every Hansom State University

Acknowledgments

This book had its origins in what I thought would be a short illustration to begin a lecture on the challenges to Christian faith experienced by Christian students attending state or other secular universities. The illustration grew so that it became half of the lecture itself. It appears here as chapter one. Chapter two is essentially the second half of that lecture. My thanks go to Wheaton College, which invited me to present this talk in the Morris Inch Lectureship, spring 1991.

Other sections of this book, especially the material on individualism and privatization and the cosmic lordship of Christ, have at least part of their origin in lectures and discussions developed for Agents of Transformation, a training program sponsored by the Great Lakes Region of InterVarsity Christian Fellowship. My thanks go first to James Paternoster, with whom I worked from the first of these programs in 1986 to the writing of this book in the summer of 1992. There are sections of the book, especially in the material on privatization, that are probably more his than mine. None of it would have been conceived without his stimulation to think about these issues.

Working with this training program was an experience of true community. No one but a rancher is more individualistic than a college professor. I had never even team-taught a course before working with the staff of Agents of Transformation. In that program we began using each other's materials, so that after a couple of years it has become difficult to know whose work is whose. I am pleased to have my own material absorbed into that of others. I hope they will be pleased to see their material absorbed into mine.

Behind the Agents of Transformation program itself lies the genius of other InterVarsity Great Lakes Region staff such as Tom Trevethan, Dan Denk and Jim Lundgren. And behind them the genius of C. Stephen Board, who worked with Tom Trevethan in the first Christian Study Project, a 1970s and early 1980s predecessor of Agents of Transformation.

Finally, I would like to acknowledge the hundreds of college students whom I have known over the past three decades. They have provided the basis for the characters who live in this book. No one character has only one source. I would like to think that many students could see themselves and their friends in Chris, Bob, Susie and the others. Any truth of character these characters display is due to their being created in the image of those who are divinely created in God's own image. Any distortion they display is due to the fallenness, finiteness and sheer incompetence of their human creator.

1
CHRIS CHRISMAN
GOES TO STATE

We believe in Marxfreudanddarwin.
We believe everything is OK
as long as you don't hurt anyone,
to the best of your definition of hurt,
and to the best of your knowledge.
(STEVE TURNER, "CREED")

*O*nce upon a time there was a student named Chris Chrisman. Chris was raised in a modestly evangelical Christian family in suburban Central City. He and his family attended church regularly, and Chris gave his life to Christ, as he would put it, the summer before he became a freshman at West Bolling High. He attended his church youth group and was the treasurer his final year. His private spiritual life consisted of more or less consistent ten-minute devotions before retiring each evening.

He knew the plan of salvation his church emphasized, he had a passing acquaintance with one Gospel, and he remembered the close reading that one of his church-school teachers had given of the book of Revelation. That fascinated him a lot, but he wasn't sure his teacher was completely right about what it all meant. The charts and graphs made the book much more specific than he thought the text itself seemed. But that was okay; his teacher had really studied it.

Chris got good grades in high school, and so two years ago he entered Hansom State University, pretty much the top university in his area. He wasn't sure what he wanted to major in, so he enrolled in the basic courses—English Comp, Introduction to Sociology, Biology 101 and World Civilization 120—that he knew would stand him well no matter what field he opted for later.

Then, to top it off, he decided to enroll in a fairly specialized course that he'd noticed on the list of electives. It was called Religious Options Around the World and was described in the catalog as "introducing Western students to the panorama of both Western and Eastern religions." What especially intrigued him was that the professor would invite guest lecturers from several major religions, some of which, like Zen, Chris had never heard of.

Once the semester began, Chris didn't have much difficulty handling the academic coursework. He found that with modest effort to stay alert in class and modest time to read and do his homework he could get more than modest grades. By the time of midterms he was relaxed and well into the swing of studies. Nothing presented in his classes seemed particularly difficult to understand. But he was beginning to sense that something odd was happening to him. And it seemed to be happening not in the classroom but in the dorm.

Chris had come to college with his Bible. He'd expected that he would continue to read it each evening and try to find some time, maybe when his roommate was out, to pray. And he did this. His roommate, Ralph Imokay, didn't mind. In fact, by the third week Chris was openly but quietly having his devotions whether his roommate was in the room or not. His roommate was, in fact, rather accommodating.

"Hey," he told Chris, "it's your life. Whatever you believe is fine with me."

As Chris soon found out, though, "whatever" did not include the idea that Ralph should believe the same thing as Chris. In fact, Ralph was not at all interested in knowing what Chris believed, let alone in believing it. Chris hadn't been pushy with his faith. In fact, before he could be, Ralph had warned him off.

"Listen," he cautioned, "what you're into is fine. But only fine for you. It doesn't have to be my thing. And it isn't. So just keep your Bible on your side of the room."

Ralph was a decent enough guy. Chris found him easy to get along with as long as he let Ralph think and do his own thing. Actually, Ralph turned out to be quite helpful when Chris got hung up on a concept in sociology he didn't understand and had to write a paper on it due the next day. He even loaned Chris a clean shirt when he came up short. In fact, it was difficult to see just how Chris's faith made him any better than this guy who, as far as Chris could tell, believed in nothing special. After all, he and Chris were really after the same things as far as school was concerned—a good job with a good company, or maybe, if things worked out right, a great job with a great company. Both were good students.

Now the others on his floor—they were a motley bunch. Chris was glad he had drawn Ralph in the great roommate lottery.

Cynthia Sharp, a sophomore who lived across the hall, was always down on Chris and every other guy in the dorm for being sexist. Chris found he could say very little without getting some disgusted retort from her. She introduced Chris to the idea of being "politically correct." She had spent a year at Buckherst College before transferring to Hansom State and now wanted to introduce all the subtleties of PC to Backwater U, as she called Hansom State. All in all, she made a peaceful life in the dorm lounge rather chancy.

Cynthia's roommate, Susie Sylvan, was a quiet and pretty freshman. Chris was immediately attracted to her; she had red hair and a few freckles and was, Chris thought, properly demure. But what, he wondered, was she was doing with a Book of Mormon among her textbooks? Chris had noticed this when, early in the semester, he had bumped into her in the hall and all her books had gone sliding down the corridor.

Down the hall was a guy, Charlie Potter, who said he was a Rastafarian, though Chris thought it was just his excuse to smoke marijuana, which he did in a stall in the john to keep the residential adviser off the track. It didn't work well, and after he was caught for the second time Charlie had to cool it. Charlie's roommate, Phil Corper, was a business major, totally oriented to getting out and getting on. Chris never heard Charlie or Phil say a word to each other.

Two of the more colorful characters were Jane and John. They roomed across the hall from each other but were always together. They could be heard in one or other of their rooms chanting "Om mane padme hum" over and over again. The aroma of incense would waft down the hall, sometimes covering the smell of pot from the guys' john. In the lounge John would throw out the strangest questions. Most of them Chris couldn't recall five minutes later, but one did stick in his mind. It had kicked off the weirdest conversation he'd ever had. "What is the sound of one hand clapping?" John mused. Then everything went up for grabs. An hour later John left with Jane to hum a few bars of Om, and Chris returned to his room and went to bed with a splitting headache.

Jane's and John's roommates—fortunately for their own sakes—were seldom around. Both were living with their lovers somewhere off campus and keeping their dorm rooms largely as mailing addresses for their parents' letters.

One thing all of the thirty students on Chris's floor had in common was that—except for the chanters—they had very little in common. There was one politically active student (a Young Republican in a Democrat-dominated university); one Methodist who never went to church; two Reformed Jews; a Catholic who had attended mass at the Newman Center every morning at 6:00 a.m. for the first month and then never attended mass again as long as he was in school; a Catholic who rarely attended mass but was always reading Thomas Merton; a couple of loud basketball players, biding their time till the season came around. Then there was Abe Knox, a Christian who wore a T-shirt emblazoned with "Knights of Jesus" in red and black; his aggressive evangelistic demeanor made Chris cringe.

Ethnic background was mixed too—blacks, Hispanics, American-born Koreans and Chinese—though predominantly white American with European roots all mixed up and long lost anyway.

It was his experience of dormitory life that gave Chris his first hint that something was changing in him. He was growing up, he was learning a lot of new things in his university classes, but after a couple of months he was beginning to feel odd.

In fact, Chris was coming apart.

The narrative that had sustained him throughout his conscious existence as a human being—that is, since he'd left adolescence behind—was coming unraveled. The world was supposed to be a place where you graduated from high school, went to college, learned which ropes to grab and pull and which to leave swinging, got introduced into a profession, found a modestly beautiful "girl" to marry a few months after college or after professional school, and then set forth to make your way as an adult. And if you were a Christian you kept the faith, let people know you believed in Christ, perhaps even led a person or two to the Lord. Life would unfold in a path that, while it might look crooked while you were on it, would look straight-arrow when you looked back. There was a meaning to life. Christ was that meaning, and one either found him or one didn't. The Christian way is the only true way, Chris had assumed. To miss it is simply to be in error. That meant one would miss a meaningful life with God on this earth, and after death, instead of experiencing a fulfilled life with God and his people, one would spend eternity in a rather unpleasant place.

This narrative didn't seem so certain now—for several reasons. The first, though, was not really so much a reason as an experience. It was all those people on his floor in his dorm, and all the others. Multiply the thirty on Chris's floor by four floors of fifteen dorms and thirty floors of five dorms. Floor after floor of individuals, each with a separate way of viewing reality. It made his head hurt. Who is right? Is anyone right? What should I believe? Isn't one thing just as good as another? Why shouldn't I live with a lover—same sex, different sex—why not? Why should I believe anything at all?

Chris now began to notice how his academic coursework was not helping to resolve these difficulties in the least. Most of them never raised the questions he was interested in. In English he struggled with a few foibles of his graduate-student English instructor, but soon learned what he wanted and produced it. It wasn't what Chris wanted.

In Biology everything went smoothly until Professor Barbara Silvera insisted that evolution by chance and necessity was a fact; design had nothing to do with it. Professor Silvera had asked on a test, "By what process did the giraffe come to have a long neck?" and Chris had answered, "In order to reach the leaves at the top of the trees." The professor's comment on that idea was devastating. Silvera's grad-student grader later explained to Chris why the professor's comment was so harsh and what it meant for evolution to be nonteleological, without deliberate direction, strictly accidental. At least that's what Chris thought it meant, though he could never quite get the hang of that notion. It didn't seem to explain what it purported to explain. But Chris couldn't quite figure out why.

Chris found out later that Professor Silvera had once chanced to be battered in a public dialogue with a creationist who, the professor said, pretended to be a scientist but was simply a misguided ideologue. Now in her class presentations she gave no consideration to any of the creationist's arguments; she just flatly denied that they were relevant. This gave Chris a funny feeling. Obviously, Professor Silvera knew biology; she talked and thought circles around the best students in the class. What she said about evolution seemed credible. Yet it went against Chris's notion of God's somehow being in charge.

Sociology didn't help either. Everything had a natural explanation, if it had one at all. Religion was the opiate of the people or the vestige of our primitive origins, a piece of the machinery of society or (and

Chris could make very little of this) a language game played in a thousand different dialects. It was anything but true. In fact, the question of religious truth seldom came up in the course; when it did— usually from a puzzled student—it was laid to rest by the comment "We do not deal with the truth or falsity of religious ideas, only with their history and function in the fabric of society. Your question is just not one sociology tries to answer."

World Civilization fascinated Chris. It introduced him not just to Western civilization but to prehistory, primal peoples, African and Asian history and a good deal more, but the course moved so fast that Chris felt like he did on his first commercial jet flight. He had looked forward to seeing the entire United States as he flew from New York to San Francisco, but he found that except for the high mountains and dry desert of the West everything was in a soft haze. So too, in World Civ a few things, like ancient Greece and Egypt, stood out, but most of the course was a big blur. Still, he did well on the many multiple-choice quizzes and the occasional short papers he had to write.

But it was the special course that had interested him at the beginning of the semester that really gave him fits. Religious Options Around the World—that was the right title, all right. That was precisely how the course was taught. Here's an option. There's an option. Here's the potted history of this option. There's the potted history of that option. (Each got a chapter in a book called *Major Religions of the World*.) Chris did like the fact that Professor Comprel asked guests from several of the religions to speak to the class. That gave each option personal credibility.

But that was the problem again. Each faith looked right to each of those who spoke, and each one began to look right to Chris as he heard them and noted their sincerity. Still, that couldn't be so if Christianity was the one true way—and that was what Chris believed. Chris tried several times to raise the question of which if any of the various faiths could be thought to be true. But Professor Comprel would not answer, and when one of the guests would make a stab at answering, the professor would soften his or her argument with something like "Remember, we are talking about religious belief here. Truth is not really the issue. It's beyond the scope of this course. And besides, in a state school we can't advocate any particular religion in a classroom." He did suggest, though, that Chris take a course in the philosophy of religion. He thought that they just might deal with the truth question there, though of course not by way of advocating any specific religion.

With all this confusion, Chris decided that discretion was the better part of valor. The advice his roommate had given him at the beginning of the semester became the principle he decided to live by—at least for a while. He would live and let live. His faith was not so much put on the back burner as confined to his private life. Among his fellow students he would take on the color of his surroundings—accede to the notion that everyone is entitled to his or her own views on anything. All notion of sharing his faith with the idea that others should be converted was laid aside. The wind had gone out of his sails, and the ship of Chris's faith lay dead in the water.[1]

stop

2
THE VORTEX
OF MODERNITY

We believe in sex before during
and after marriage.
We believe in the therapy of sin.
We believe that adultery is fun.
We believe that sodomy's OK
We believe that taboos are taboo.
(STEVE TURNER, "CREED")

What has happened to Chris Chrisman?

Chris Chrisman has been done to. He has been sucked into the vortex of the modern university, where whirl is king. Chris has faced the challenges the university poses for Christian faith, and already, at the end of his first semester in college, he has lost his grip.

Let's leave the story of Chris and his friends for a while and look at the forces that have moved against his faith. This will be the first of several chapters in which I invite the reader to step back from the story and think with me about the issues it raises.

In this chapter we will look first at the sociological and then the intellectual forces that are working on Chris, mostly without his knowing it. He could, of course, learn about these forces, and as the story progresses we will find him doing so.

Four Forces of Modernity

Every human being is enmeshed in society and, more broadly, in culture. We are social beings. We began that way as children, growing up in one specific family and one specific country, learning one specific language (some grow up speaking two from childhood) and being governed by a specific social order. Our first beliefs are those of our first environment, usually our parents. We are shaped socially and psychologically before we know what our shape is.

Sometime in adolescence we begin to know ourselves as ourselves. We begin to recognize who we are and begin to have some ability consciously to shape who we will be from then on. But we never lose our rootedness. We never become autonomous individuals totally in charge of who we are and who we will be.

Chris Chrisman could have rebelled against his upbringing, but he never felt much like doing so. Those in his high school who did rebel were known in Chris's crowd as punkers or deadheads.

Begin Let's briefly survey a few of the forces that were working on Chris even after he had achieved some degree of self-identity, some measure of autonomy. Sociologists label this complex of forces *modernity:* the condition of modern society. Most of them will be addressed in greater detail in subsequent chapters.

Individualism

Individualism is at the root of modernity. Individualism proclaims, "I am self-sufficient. I need not, I ought not, depend on anyone but myself. After all, I am who I am; I am who I make myself to be."

Individualism is primarily a Western phenomenon. It is rooted in the Christian notion of being created in the image of God. But it appears in its modern form, if not first, then certainly most visibly in Martin Luther's refusal to agree with the hierarchy of the church. "Unless I am convicted by Scripture and plain reason, I will not change my mind." The individual conscience cannot be forced.

Chris himself felt this way—especially as he found himself with others who disagreed with him. Had he looked at his situation historically, he would have discovered that he was an heir of John Locke, Ben Franklin and Walt Whitman.

With John Locke, for example, the individual is the fundamental reality. Society is secondary. Society is formed by a social contract between its individual members. The idea is that each person's ego boundaries (who one essentially is) end with the skin. I am I. You are you. We are separate beings. We are not part of one another. I can and will pursue my own interests, and I will measure my success by my material possessions, my social power and my prestige. Moreover, I will express myself against all constraints, all traditions. "I gotta be me!"

Who are our heroes? John Wayne, Ernest Hemingway, Lee Iacocca, Sylvester Stallone (Rambo, Rocky), Horatio Alger, Sam Spade, Shane, Han Solo, Indiana Jones, Humphrey Bogart and Clint Eastwood. Chris, though not a Lutheran, had long thought Martin Luther a very great man. Back in his church youth group he'd seen a well-acted film on Luther's stand against the corruption of truth.

Pluralism

Pluralism is multiple-choice lifestyle. That was life at Hansom State University with a vengeance. With individualism at the helm of society, what else could emerge than a grab bag of values? Pluralism, in fact, has become one of the central features of the Western world. With each turn of the earth, so it seems, a host of new forms of belief and practice are sown and take root virtually unhindered.

To the more or less unified Christian worldview of the Middle Ages was gradually added a wide variety of protesting Christian faiths—German Lutheranism, Genevan Calvinism, English via media, Anabaptist separatism, et cetera, ad infinitum. To the varieties of Protestantism were added the skepticism of intellectuals like Montaigne and the exaltation of Reason in the Enlightenment. Eventually belief in God was eroded, naturalism became dominant in Western universities, and Christianity took a gradually shrinking role in shaping the cultural norms of society.

By the end of the nineteenth century Eastern thought was penetrating the West as Indian, Japanese and Chinese philosophy and religion became known and attractive to more and more people. By the mid-twentieth century, in most Western countries there was hardly a philosophy or religious practice that was not represented by a major spokesperson or religious group. Today Chris's college roommate could have been anything from an atheist to a pre-Vatican II Catholic, Zen Buddhist, Rastafarian, neopagan or Hindu.

No religion is dominant in culture at large; none is authoritative; yet each of them is viable. To raise the question of which of them is true is to violate social mores. That brings us to the next social force.

Relativism

The third social force we experience is *relativism*. Faced by multiple options, the West has decided to make social peace by refusing to question the truth of each of its religious and philosophic perspectives. "It's true for you. Okay. But it isn't true for me and it doesn't have to be."

Ralph Imokay, Chris's roommate, said it well. "Look," he told Chris for the third time, "I'm okay. You're okay. And that's okay. Okay?" After that it was.

In Chris's religion class and in the dorm too, religious statements—whether historical ("On the third day Jesus rose from the dead") or theological ("God was in Christ reconciling the world to himself")—were considered *beliefs*, not claims to *truth*. They were neither true nor false.

Ethical values were treated in the same way. It's okay for you to believe that abortion is wrong, but it's also okay for me to believe it is not. "It's okay for me to get drunk on Friday night and sleep it off Saturday. It's okay for you to be a teetotaler. It's not okay for you to bug me about what's my business only." That's the way one of Chris's dormmates put it.

Of course, there are still many secular humanists, many Christians and many Muslims who take truth claims seriously. But they are out of step with the direction of modernity. They act like flavor centers in a great amorphous pudding, but they do not give a pervasive flavor to the pluralistic mix itself.

Privatization

The fourth force of modernity is *privatization*. This is simply the tendency for social reality to be split into two sectors: the public and the private. In the *public* sector are matters of government, politics, business, economics, production, technology, science. This realm is governed by *fact*. Facts are, of course, determined by reason as expressed primarily in the scientific method. If you can prove it by the canons of science, it is true—a fact. This is the orderly world of the public domain; there is little freedom of movement here. The business world determines whom it will employ: if you fit you're in; if you don't you're not.

In the *private* sector are matters of religion, morality, leisure, consumption. You are not required to believe any particular doctrine, attend any particular church, go to any particular sporting event or buy any particular product. There is much "personal" freedom here. So much so, in fact, that one's ideas and preferences are matters of choice, perhaps just of "taste." Facts are not relevant; *beliefs* are your own business, and there is no public check on them. You can believe anything you want. There is no right or wrong.

These are only a few of the social forces acting on Chris and other Christians who attend secular universities. We could add professionalization, bureaucratization, specialization, technologization. Combine these with shifts in worldview from theism to naturalism, pantheism and various versions of New Age thought, and you have a sense of what any Christian is up against.

Naturalism

Chris was also being besieged by intellectual forces. Ideas have consequences: they shape and reshape lives. Chris was being reshaped by naturalism, still the reigning worldview on secular university campuses.

Except for Religious Options Around the World, every course Chris took was taught by a person who, like his biology instructor, either did not believe any God existed or, like his sociology instructor, never even hinted at what he or she personally believed. His religion prof, Professor Comprel, seemed to think that every religion was fine, regardless of whether it upheld faith in God.

Moreover, and more important, the courses themselves moved through their content without ever using God as a factor. Sociology never considered that God might be the source of the idea of God; rather, the idea of God came from such things as primitive longings for meaning, imaginative constructs of ingenious poets and ethical mechanisms for physical survival.

"The cosmos is all there is or ever was or ever will be," said Carl Sagan.[1]

This sentence is the briefest possible definition of naturalism. Naturalism holds that everything that exists is on its own and that all explanations are naturalistic explanations. All mystery is simply complexity we don't yet understand. "We now know that we exist by evolutionary accident, as one species among many, on a small and insignificant world in one little corner of the cosmos," says philosopher James Rachels.[2]

This presumption undergirds the primary theories and practices of every academic discipline, including (for the most part) the field of religion. The natural scientists assume that their theories are based on facts recognized as such by their competent peers.

Many human scientists try to imitate the procedures of the hard sciences, but with considerably less consensus even among themselves as to the results. Other human scientists build their theories on less stable data and view their results with much more skepticism. Those in the humanities—except for philosophy—just chart patterns of ideas, bask in the aesthetic beauty of their subjects and exult in the many-splendored multiplicity of images, stories, ideas, sights and sounds. Some, like Paul de Man and Jacques Derrida, cleverly deconstruct the very soul of intelligence—the language we use to apprehend meaning.

Only philosophy remains to ask the big questions: Is it true? Is it good? How can we know? Some naturalist philosophers have not abandoned reason. Moreover, some Christians have stood out—among them Nicholas Wolterstorff, Alvin Plantinga, William Alston, Keith Yandell, George Mavrodes, Arthur Holmes and C. Stephen Evans.

But even philosophy contains within its ranks those who have abandoned the search for truth. Richard Rorty, for example, believes the best society we can have is "one which is content to call 'true' (or 'right' or 'just') whatever the outcome of undistorted communication happens to be, whatever view wins in a free and open encounter."[3] Rorty ends up commending the poets rather than the scientists and philosophers, not because they lead us to truth but because they give us a thrill:

> If you want to be remembered by future generations, go in for poetry rather than for mathematics. If you want your books to be read rather than respectfully shrouded in tooled leather, you should try to produce tingles rather than truth. What we call common sense—the body of widely accepted truths—is, just as Heidegger and Nabokov thought, a collection of dead metaphors. Truths are the skeletons which remain after the capacity to arouse the senses—to cause tingles—has been rubbed off by familiarity and long usage.[4]

With naturalism as the overwhelmingly dominant worldview in the secular university, Christians and religious people of every stamp are going to have difficulty keeping their faith.

Many over the past two centuries have not. They have simply capitulated and become naturalists.

New Spiritualities

Others have not so much accommodated to the shifting permutations of naturalist-oriented thought as gone beyond it into New Age thinking.

In New Age thought, the self of each person is seen to be the center of reality. All of reality is permeated by spirit, and the central spirit of all is one's own self. On the popular level, New Agers include such celebrities as Shirley MacLaine and John Denver. Among spiritual leaders there is the Maharishi Mahesh Yogi with his Transcendental Meditation (TM for short).

Because the New Age majors in experience and tends to downgrade anything highly intellectual, it is somewhat surprising to see that it has gained a significant following even on university campuses. A prime example of New Age thought on campus can even be found among the academic theologians. Thomas C. Oden put aside traditional Christianity and went on a long, winding search for spiritual reality.[5]

Oden, in fact, describes himself as a "movement person." "In his pursuit of movements, his overall pattern was diligently to learn from them, to throw himself into them, and eventually to baptize them as they showed any remote kinship with Christianity, and then to turn to another movement." At age sixteen he joined a movement to promote world government; his interests then flowed from ecumenism and involvement with the NAACP (in 1953) on to pacifist activism during the Vietnam War. He was associated with the American Civil Liberties Union and the pre-NOW women's rights movement as an advocate of liberalized abortion. In the late 1950s he "became enamored with the existentialist movement, immersing himself particularly in the demythologization movement, writing his doctoral dissertation on its chief theorist" (Bultmann). In the early sixties he took up client-centered therapy and then moved on to Transactional Analysis and Gestalt therapy, "especially through Esalen [New Age] connections." He taught from these perspectives in theological classrooms.

This was supplemented by several years of involvement in the T-

Group movement associated with the National Training Laboratories, which he tried to integrate into his religious views. In the early 1970s, he joined a society for the study of paranormal phenomena, taught a class in parapsychology, and directed controlled research experiments with mung beans, Kirlian photography, biorhythm charts, pyramids, tarot cards, and the correlation of astrological predictions with the daily ups and downs of behavior.

It was only after *Roe* v. *Wade* that he came to his senses. "It was the abortion-on-demand movement more than anything else that brought me to movement revulsiveness." Oden experienced a conversion of sorts and returned to the roots of his faith, the Bible and its interpreters in the first thousand years of church history. He is now back among the orthodox, calling for a "postcritical" theology, one that knows the history of culture and thought and takes a muscular stance on the truth of God's revelation in Christ.

Thomas Oden survived as a Christian. Will Chris Chrisman survive? What will happen as the semesters unfold and Chris approaches graduation and perhaps stays on for graduate school or professional school?

And what of those who come to the university with what they think of as no faith at all? Are they in better shape?

3
BOB WONG
GOES TO STATE

We believe that after death comes The Nothing
because when you ask the dead what happens
they say Nothing.
If death is not the end, if the dead have lied,
then it's compulsory heaven for all
excepting perhaps Hitler, Stalin and Genghis Khan.
(STEVE TURNER, "CREED")

*B*ob Wong began his university career at the same time as Chris Chrisman. But though their paths crossed during the first semester, neither one knew it.

Bob came to State from out of state. In fact, Bob was born in Taiwan and moved with his parents to California when he was only three. Sometimes in a recurring dream Bob sees a little boy in a strange place running through a forest of legs, looking lost and beginning to cry. The setting of the dream reminds him of Chinatown in San Francisco. But Bob grew up in Mendocino, a beautiful tourist village a hundred miles north of San Francisco. So Bob thinks his dream—which more and more has taken on a nightmarish quality—shows his deep link to his Chinese heritage.

That's why the dream is a nightmare. Bob would give anything to be rid of his Chinese roots. He wants to be one hundred percent American—dress American, think American, live American, look

American. He has largely succeeded. His parents wanted to come to the States but have felt comfortable retaining most of their Chinese cultural values, and they have tried to transmit these to their family. But Bob has long been a sadness to them. By third grade, Bob began to realize that even though he enjoyed exactly the same things as his friends, they treated him a bit differently. By fifth grade he knew why, and by seventh grade he was determined to erase from himself every vestige of his Chinese heritage. For the most part, this was not difficult. All he had to do was be with his friends, do what they did, participate in their lives. And this he did with the determination of a high-school athlete training for the Olympics. Like a star athlete, Bob enjoyed every minute of his regimen.

One vestige of his heritage he was easily rid of. His parents were Buddhists, modestly practicing the faith of their forebears. They had a family altar with photographs of their ancestors, and there was fruit and burning incense, though his parents were more or less perfunctory in their worship.

Some people in Mendocino and the mountains above the town also claimed to be Buddhist, but Bob's family soon saw that their Buddhism was a mixed bag of Zen—not the tradition from which they came (and if anything more Japanese than Buddhist, as far as they could tell)—watered-down Hinduism and nondescript aestheticism. They were endlessly writing poetry and reading it to each other and anyone else who would listen. But there were no Buddhist "churches" in Mendocino, and his parents did not choose to travel often to San Francisco, where they could participate in authentic Buddhist worship. Besides, even in Taiwan they hadn't been particularly devout. They were lured by the West, by the economic opportunity they saw in America, and they did not think of their religious roots as tying them to their homeland.

Bob's father and mother had both been children of families that had fled to Taiwan from mainland China long ago. Bob was not quite sure which set of violent events had triggered that; he just wasn't interested enough to learn, or to remember when he did learn. The Boxer Rebellion, the Long March, the Japanese occupation and the Cultural Revolution all swam vaguely together in his mind. Bob didn't know it, but he had become a child of America, a child of Henry Ford: "History is bunk."

While Bob quickly abandoned the faith of his parents, he did not pick up the faith of the beat generation either. He was born too late for that and too early to be enticed by the growing interest in Americanized New Age spirituality. No, Bob vowed he would have nothing to do with religion whatsoever. It was a serious vow.

Bob became an atheist before he knew he was an atheist. He had rejected all the religiosity of his parents and had been totally unimpressed by anything he had heard from his friends who went to church. He himself had never been to church. There didn't seem to be much reason to go. His friends who did attend church were required to do so by their parents, and as far as Bob knew none of them had even a private faith, let alone a public one.

Except for Hank. Now he was different. He went to a small church a few miles up into the mountains. Hank was a Christian. Boy, was he! And an evangelist. He was always inviting the high-school kids to revival meetings. "You've got to be saved if you don't want to go to hell," he would tell people—endlessly. Hank didn't have many friends. A few younger students used to hang around with him, but that was about all. Bob tried to have nothing to do with him and succeeded.

Bob found out he was an atheist when he met Michael Stone. Michael had known he was an atheist for a long time, having grown up in a secular Jewish family with a long heritage of intellectual sophistication. And Michael was not rebelling. Michael was a young man with intellectual promise, as his father kept telling his mother, and found his family's secular "faith" attractive. In fact, he was an evangelist for it. His family had long ago kicked over the benighted literalism of Orthodox Judaism. They had come into the Enlightened—yes, with a capital *E*—twentieth century. Einstein would have been their hero if he hadn't believed in some benign "mind" permeating the universe. No, the cosmos was just there—no reason for it. The only reason was human reason, and that was quite adequate for all we human beings need to be and do. Evolution brought us here, not for any purpose but just because that's the way it worked out when the impersonal forces of the universe did their thing.

Bob and Michael both played chess, Bob because he liked it and Michael because it was what young intellectuals were supposed to do and he wanted to fulfil his destiny. Besides, he liked it too.

Endless hours the two spent together, heads bent over a chessboard, minds battling out their philosophies as well as their strategies and tactics. Pawn to king four put their minds in gear. And though Bob proved the slightly better chess player, Michael thought circles around Bob—at least their first year together. By the time they graduated from high school, Bob could hold his own in a philosophic argument. Always, however, they argued about details. Both began as atheists and ended four years later as atheists.

Then they both went to college. Michael was ecstatic to get accepted at Bertrand College, an exclusive private school known for its academic rigor.

Bob had very different plans. His parents would have loved to have him join Michael at Bertrand. It had an excellent reputation for getting its graduates into the best professional schools. But Bob was not interested in law or medicine or even business. He wanted to pursue his own quest.

It had taken hours of negotiation with his parents over many days, but finally Bob had secured their reluctant permission to do what he really wanted.

Bob had been looking at college catalogs and a map. Hansom State was, he thought, ideal. It was thousands of miles away; it was a good but undistinguished school (that is, there were many schools just as prestigious, and many more so); and it offered Bob what he wanted—

a ticket away from the West Coast and into the center of America. *What can be more American than the Midwest?* he thought.

So Bob Wong went to State.

Bob enrolled in English Comp, World Civ, Biology—the same courses as Chris Chrisman, but different sections. And he took Religious Options Around the World with Professor Comprel. He thought that because this was a university, certainly the teacher would not be a believer in any of the religions he taught. He would be too intelligent. Taking a course on this topic from an atheist professor would round out Bob's critique of all religions and forever justify his own atheistic commitment—not that Bob had any doubts about it.

Then a curious thing happened. Bob began to have the same experience as Chris. Like Chris, Bob lived in a coed dorm. In the luck of the draw, however, Bob's roommate turned out to be a Christian. Kevin Leaver had arrived on campus just before Bob and had unpacked first. When Bob arrived, there on the desk was a big black Bible. Bob almost panicked. Then Kevin walked in and introduced himself. Bob saw him as friendly but shy. They exchanged a few details about themselves, and Bob relaxed. Actually, he discovered, Kevin was a pretty nice guy. And what amazed Bob the most was that he seemed intelligent. He was premed, and Bob could see he was confident about going all the way through med school. Bob would find out later that Kevin was the valedictorian of his high school and there were six hundred in his graduating class.

Then there were the others on their floor: a couple of first-year women who hung around Kevin a lot because they too were Christians, a young man from Sri Lanka who was a Buddhist, several guys who were obviously Jewish but not so interested in intellectual pursuits as Michael, and an assortment of nondescript others whom Bob only gradually came to know. None of them were atheists.

Halfway through the semester, Bob, like Chris, was coming apart at the seams.

All these people in the dormitory—all these intelligent people: why did they still believe in God, or at least in some higher being? Only his biology professor—Dr. Darwin, the students called him; his name was really Darwain—admitted to being an atheist. Even the grad-student lab instructor was unwilling to do that. He would say to people troubled by evolution, "Look, God could've done it that way. It's just that we can't do science by using God as an explanation. So let's stick with what we can know from the physical facts before us." Then he would explain evolution just like Dr. Darwain.

Professor Comprel gave him the most trouble. Why was he so sympathetic to so many beliefs? Couldn't he see that they contradicted each other? In high school Michael Stone had taught Bob the basics of logic. X and not-X could not both be true. Zen Buddhism taught that there was no personal higher being; Islam said there was. Comprel thought both had something true to say but neither was final. That, as far as Bob was concerned, was nonsense, but when he made an objection along those lines in class Comprel said, "You must look for the truth within the statements, behind the words. The truth here is symbolic." Well, Bob concluded, if that was so he had certainly better not major in symbolism, because he couldn't see truth of any kind behind two sentences that contradicted each other.

Bob had indeed become immersed in the university mind—individualistic, pluralistic, relativistic, privatized. He was losing his grip on his atheism. He was in trouble.

Bob was beginning to doubt his atheism. All the machinations of Professor Comprel, all the conversations he'd had in the dorm, especially with his roommate, were getting to him. His roommate had not come on like Hank back in Mendocino. Like Chris, Kevin had a simple faith and knew enough to know that it takes just as much faith to believe that God doesn't exist as it does to believe that he does. Bob was gradually coming to believe this too. But he still didn't believe that Kevin's faith could be true. That seemed too much like a leap in the dark.

"Okay, maybe I can't prove God doesn't exist," he told Kevin at the peak of a heated argument, "but you can't prove he does either, and the whole God thing looks pretty unlikely to me." Then he paused and said, "Maybe Comprel is right. Maybe it doesn't make any difference what you believe. Maybe any belief, if you're serious about it, is just as good as any other."

Modernity cuts both ways. It slays belief and unbelief alike—Christian faith and atheism, Buddhism and Hinduism, Islam and Judaism. If all of these could be true for some and not true for others, the ground shakes beneath us, opens up and pitches us into a sea of infinite possibility where no north star shines to tell us where we are.

So both Chris Chrisman and Bob Wong were at sea. Neither of them knew quite where they were. Misery may love company, but sometimes company salves misery. What would happen if Chris and Bob should meet?

Hot point

4
CHRIS CHRISMAN BECOMES A STUDENT

We believe in Masters and Johnson.
What's selected is average.
What's average is normal.
What's normal is good.
(STEVE TURNER, "CREED")

C hris Chrisman went through the last few weeks of his first semester in a fog. He went home for Thanksgiving and didn't have much to say to his parents about what was going on in his mind.

"How are you getting along in school?" his mother asked.

"Oh, fine."

"Are you finding the courses difficult?"

"No. Not really. Well, I did at first, but I caught on pretty soon. I think my grades will be okay."

"How do you like your roommate?"

"Oh, Ralph? He's okay. Yeah, we get along fine. We don't do a lot together, but we've worked out the rough spots. He's kind of meticulous, and I've had to keep my room a little neater than I had expected. Gosh, Mom, I think you'll like that little change in me."

"Have you met any nice girls?"

Now there was a loaded question. Chris pretty much knew what his mother meant by "nice." He was glad he could say he really hadn't met any college women he'd gotten to know much. There was only Susie, the attractive redhead across the hall, and he didn't want to get involved with a Mormon. So Chris said nothing.

"Have you been going to church?" she asked.

"Oh, yeah. There's a church a lot like ours here at home. I take a bus on Sunday mornings, and I've gone quite a few times."

Actually, Chris had gone almost every Sunday. What he didn't tell his mother, though, was that nothing at the church was helping him with his deteriorating Christian conviction. The sermons had been okay but irrelevant to his questions. The Sunday-school class was studying Moses; the teacher did most of the talking and Chris found his own mind wandering more than the Israelites in the desert.

Chris talked with his father too, and the conversation went pretty much the same except that his father added a couple of questions: "Have you chosen a major yet?" and "What are you planning to do after you graduate?" His father was also interested in how much money Chris thought he would need for books and other expenses during the next term.

After Chris went back to State, he immersed himself in his studies and the semester closed out quickly. He didn't have much time to think about what was troubling his spirit. That didn't really occur again till Christmas.

And Christmas break did prove unsettling. Chris was not troubled by the usual frustration Christians express (but don't really have)—the commercialism and the distraction of visiting relatives. Chris was, rather, troubled by the "real meaning of Christmas."

Did God become a human being in a manger twelve thousand miles away and two thousand years ago? Did this birth signal a new age? Did Jesus really come to take away the sins of the world? Chris remembered the Scripture he had heard read in his college church. It was Mary's song:

He has performed mighty deeds with his arm;
> he has scattered those who are proud in their inmost thoughts.
He has brought down rulers from their thrones
> but has lifted up the humble. (Lk 1:51-52)

Has God really done this? Chris thought. "Couldn't all this just be a product of imagination, the meandering invention of an overly hopeful clever religious writer?" his sociology teacher might say. "How do we know what Mary thought or said?" All those other religions he had learned about—were they wrong? They had to be if this Christmas thing was right. But could they be? Why would so many people be so mistaken for so long a time? Jesus came so long ago that the whole world should be Christian by now. But it certainly wasn't. The university itself was proof of that. To Chris the whole Christian thing now seemed illogical, unreal.

As Christmas approached, the acids of modernity that had already eaten deeply into Chris's thought life ate all the way through his protective shield of faith.

Still, Chris went through the motions of Christian practice. He took Communion on Christmas Eve; he even believed as he took the bread and wine that what he was doing was exactly what he should be doing. And for a while he felt good. But the effects of the ceremony soon wore off, and Chris's second state was worse than the first.

After Christmas Chris went skiing up in the mountains with some of his old high-school buddies. Some had gone to different colleges; some had begun working. But they had a good time together. Chris especially, because the conversation never turned either to Christian stuff on the one hand or to anything thoughtful at all. "Girls" were high on the discussion agenda, and Chris just listened—listened with lots of attention, I might add, because he had begun to think that if he could just find a "girlfriend" that would take his mind off the troubling stuff, maybe forever. *You never know,* Chris mused, *this romance thing, this doing stuff together—it might be the way to go.*

So Chris headed back to college with a firm resolve to locate a young woman—Chris had to revert back to the proper language in his mind now that he was back in school—and get into a "meaningful relationship." Chris wasn't after sex, not yet at least. But he was after something that would permanently take his mind off what his mind was always on—intellectual woolgathering, puzzling over his faith.

He decided, too, not to read his Bible anymore. It just kept his attention on his troubles. He'd continue to go to church. That would make his parents happy.

Chris did not think this would be hard, because he was taking a new set of courses and none of them directly involved religion. But as the semester began, Chris realized that he had chosen his new courses in the throes of his puzzling thoughts. His second-semester biology and World Civ courses were no problem, but the other two courses were Philosophy 101 and English 102.

Introduction to Philosophy plunged right in where Chris had left off the previous semester. What is the really real? How can anyone know anything at all? What is the good life? His English instructor, another grad student, had chosen *Zen and the Art of Motorcycle Maintenance* as the literary text they would be reading and writing papers about for the whole semester.

Chris felt that he had leaped from the frying pan into the fire. The moment he thought that, though, he felt the pangs of his newly forming rhetorical conscience: *I'm thinking in clichés. Is there no hope for me? I don't know what I believe anymore. I can't form a coherent thought in my head. And now I'm thinking in clichés! It's enough to make my head spin.* When he reflected on *that* cliché, Chris was sure he was lost. *This semester is going to be worse than the first.*

But Chris couldn't have been more mistaken. The very first day in philosophy class, Professor Knock began talking about philosophy as the love of truth, and he read from one of Plato's dialogues. Chris had never heard such stuff before, and he was fascinated. In English class, the grad-student instructor turned out to be interested in philosophy too. In fact, he was doing his dissertation on philosophical themes in science fiction.

But most important, Chris met Bill Seipel the first day of his philosophy class. Bill came a couple of minutes after Chris, looked around the room, saw Chris, smiled, saw Chris smiling back and took the seat next to him. Bill was as fascinated by the first class session as Chris, and when the two left the room they headed for the student union for coffee and donuts.

Chris found out that Bill had just transferred to State after a semester at Cornton College, which Chris knew to be Christian with a capital *C.* Man, you couldn't even go to movies there until a couple of years ago. Bill had not come to State to escape the narrow confines of a fundamentalist school. Quite frankly, he just hadn't had the money to continue. So State looked like a good option and he took it. Bill was a first-year student, too, and it wasn't long before he and Chris became great friends.

What capped off their friendship, however, was Bill's straightforward approach to his faith. Bill was not arrogant about his beliefs, nor was he defensive. He took them in stride and tried to make them work in relation to the courses he was taking. He had already had a course at Cornton that covered some of the same issues as the philosophy class he and Chris were now taking. That course, called Introduction to the Christian Faith, had been taught by Professor Nancy Bright, a young Ph.D. who had a philosophical bent and in fact had an undergraduate degree in philosophy from Princeton. So Bill had been introduced to a thoughtful kind of Christian faith. He'd had lots of heavy conversations with Bright, especially after she found out that Bill was having to transfer to State.

Chris had finally found someone who was interested in the same questions he was. After the first week of classes Chris spelled out his frustrations as much as he could in words. Bill, exposed in the dormitory and classrooms to the same atmosphere as Chris, could see why Chris felt that way. Unlike Chris, though, he had been told about the dominant worldview at State and had discussed with Professor Bright some of the problems he might have.

Those conversations, however, had been no match for the reality of the university. Bill now could see and feel the pressures to conform to lifestyles that at Cornton people talked about but never lived—or lived only in fantasy. Bill was taking the comparative religion course Chris had taken, and he was also studying psychology and chemistry as well as taking English Comp. But Bill's special text was different. He was having to read *The Sailor Who Fell from Grace with the Sea* and write papers on postmodernity, whatever in the world that was—he had not heard of it at Cornton.

His grad-student instructor, Mr. Cod, was interested in deconstruction, and though he promised not to bring his grad work into the classroom, the word *deconstruction* began to crop up more and more frequently in the instructor's sidelong comments. The word tended to pop up when something went wrong in the class or when Mr. Cod wanted to regain control by saying something no students could understand but felt that they had to or flunk. Bill finally came to see this as the instructor's way of intimidating his students. Bill suspected that Mr. Cod was not as sure of himself as he pretended.

In any case, Bill found himself in the same muddy waters as Chris. He had had a few instructions on land about what to do if he fell in the river while steering his frail canoe, and he had put on the life preserver of steady faith. But now his canoe had capsized and he was swimming. He was delighted to have someone to swim with, someone heading in the same direction, or at least trying to.

A couple of weeks into the semester, Chris and Bill had just about talked out their mutual frustrations. They were aware of the challenge to their Christian faith. Despite his earlier resolution, Chris had actually not stopped reading the Bible and having devotions. Bill and he decided to study the same book and compare notes as they went along. They chose the Gospel of Mark. They knew that the scholars cited in the religion department had dated Mark as the first and maybe the most reliable of the Gospels (though, of course, it was a product of a church that wanted to justify its structure and power and couldn't really be taken at face value). Bill still believed the Bible, of course, and Chris was more than willing to give Scripture a chance to re-prove itself to him.

But soon Chris and Bill decided to do something else: to tackle head-on the problems both of them were facing. So at the end of that second week, they tried to identify as precisely as they could just what was bugging them about the university atmosphere. What was really eating away at their confidence in the Christian faith?

They made a list that looked something like this:

☐ No one cares whether anything is true or not. (For the moment they had forgotten about Professor Knock.)

☐ Anything is okay as long as someone thinks it's okay.

☐ There are many ways to view reality, and each of them is as viable as any other.

☐ We ought to open our minds to multiple lifestyles. Gay is good. Nongay is okay, but only if the nongay says gay is good. No one cares if we believe that Jesus is the only way to God; we just aren't supposed to tell anyone.

☐ There really isn't anything valuable to be learned in college except what's connected to good grades or a degree. The goal of education is to get a better job than we could have if we did not have a degree.

☐ What's really important is to develop our own potential.

☐ We are responsible only to ourselves for what we do.

☐ We will improve the world by improving ourselves.

☐ What we do in private is our own concern and no one else's. We ought to keep our religious beliefs private.

To Chris and Bill it seemed that some of these items contradicted others. If everything really is okay, then nongay and even antigay should be just as good as progay. But on campus it wasn't. Likewise, if one believed in private that one's private views were universal, then they could no more be reasonably kept private.

As Chris and Bill contemplated this list, they came to see that one of their problems was that they disagreed with almost every item on it. Their faith could not be kept private. Some things *were* right or wrong regardless of whether anyone thought so. They just were. The goal of education had to be more than a job. We are all responsible to God. What is really important is that what we do is approved by God. We might have to be like Jesus and give our life for our beliefs.

Christianity, as they understood it, committed them to these views. It is one of those exclusive belief systems that Prof Comprel kept shoving to the margins in his classes. He called it "exclusivist." Chris and Bill concluded that on this matter, at least, Comprel was right. Christianity *is* exclusive.

The point, though, is not whether it is exclusive but whether it is true. But that brought them back to the list again. The first item said it all: No one cared whether anything was true or not.

They didn't know it, but what they had done in making this list was to identify some of the characteristics of *modernity:* relativism, individualism, pluralism and privatization. What they did know was that they had to do something about the items on the list.

They knew they couldn't tackle all of them at once, but they also knew that the lead item seemed all-embracing. So they went after it. They decided to ask their philosophy professor if they could write their term papers on relativism. Chris would write his paper on Allan Bloom's views in *The Closing of the American Mind,* and Bill would take up the views of Lesslie Newbigin in *The Gospel in a Pluralist Society.*

Their professor was well aware of Bloom's views, but he had never heard of Newbigin. When Bill explained that he had heard about Newbigin from a professor last semester (he didn't say that this was a religion prof at a Christian college), the professor approved the topic.

When a classmate, till then unknown to them, overheard this request, he introduced himself as Bob Wong, and all three headed to the union for a Coke and a three-way conversation on Chris and Bill's most puzzling question.[1]

5
TRUTH: A MOBILE ARMY OF METAPHORS

We believe that all religions are basically the same
at least the one that we read was.
They all believe in love and goodness.
They only differ on matters of
creation sin heaven hell God and salvation.
(STEVE TURNER, "CREED")

What Chris Chrisman, Bob Wong and Bill Seipel had selected as their target topic was both academic and personal, a happy but infrequent coincidence in university education. Some students never experience it, which is to say that some students never become students.

Let's leave them to their intellectual machinations for a moment and look at the topic they have lit on—or, better, that has lit on them. Relativism is one of the most pervasive social and intellectual forces acting on university campuses today. The discussion in this and the following chapter will, therefore, be somewhat more complex than in other chapters in this book. The topic merits it; in fact, a less complex treatment would be too superficial to be helpful.[1]

The Problem Posed
A few years ago I gave a lectture at Bates College in Maine on Chris-

tianity and the university. I referred to John Henry Cardinal Newman and argued that a genuinely Christian approach to university study should see everything as created by a reasonable, rational God. This would provide the basis for a unified view of the universe, of God and human beings. I did not say we would know everything perfectly; but I was optimistic about knowing at least some things truly.[2]

The following day a formal response was given by three people. One of the respondents was a professor of philosophy. Her remarks were sharp and to the point.

"Well, I'm an academic. I am not a Christian," she began. Then she went on to give openness the highest place in the university: "Everything is up for grabs; no ideas are beyond question. No one should ever believe that they have the truth. Those who think they do have the truth are surely wrong, for no one has the truth or can have it."

Later I debated the issue of ethical norms with residence-hall directors at the University of New Hampshire. When I posed the problem of conflicting or contradictory religious claims, some maintained that a religious statement could be "true for you but not for me." Others were willing to say that was not the case; about six out of thirty said that they did not believe God existed and that my belief in him did not change the situation. Others—especially a hall director from North Carolina, raised in a conservative church—seemed not to understand what was going on in the discussion.

The setting for this verbal clash is significant: a secular school where rapes were frequent and dormitory discipline a serious problem. Students were refusing to abide by common decency. After all, why should they have to heed the rules of others?

Before we look at specific ways relativism is expressed, it is important to elaborate on one distinction.

The Fact-Value Dichotomy
A major factor in relativism is a distinction our culture has been drawing between *facts* and *values,* a distinction that has been be-

queathed to us by the Enlightenment.[3]

Facts, as we understand them, are certain, scientific and public. They are determined by scientific method—evidence and reason. In the natural sciences there is great optimism about the possibility of finding out how the universe is put together. For example, much hope is held out for unlocking the structure of the human genetic system and for positive human engineering. This optimism is extended to the hope for technological solutions to human problems, perhaps all human problems.

The realm of science is largely considered to be the realm of fact. Facts of a scientific sort can be found. The category of true-or-false applies. But the realm of fact does not extend beyond the limited regions of natural science—not, for example, into the realm of religious belief, ethical norms and values. There is indeed a fact-value dichotomy, a split that expresses itself in the general silence of the university on values and norms.

Values—beliefs about what is worthy and unworthy, good and evil— reside, unlike facts, in the radical subjectivity of a believer. Value is private. It is not determined by reason but by choice, and since we live in a world where "God is dead," there is no limit on our choice. Everything is in principle permitted.

Perhaps most problematic is the tacit assumption in the humanities and social sciences that there are no absolutes, no ultimate values. Values are the creation of human beings and human culture; they are not found in any reality outside the human frame. They are subject solely to human consciousness, human choice. So in most academic disciplines students are left to develop their own philosophy of life, as if one outlook were as good as another and no one had a leg up in this area.

If values do not come from outside the human frame, where do they come from? After Nietzsche, the answer has primarily been *the individual self.* The self—"the mysterious, free, unlimited center of our being"—is seen to be the source of value. There is no repository of value from which the self draws. The chief reason the self is seen as the repository of value is simple: Either God does not exist or his existence makes no practical difference.

Recent polls suggest that a very great majority of Americans believe in the existence of God.[4] But both their actions and their words on other matters betray them. God is indeed dead or dying in our culture.

If the God of Abraham, Isaac and Jacob and the Father of our Lord Jesus Christ does in fact exist, then he is the source and determiner of the good. We do not then have "values" but "goodness" itself as a standard of righteousness. But our culture more and more ignores its stated belief in God. We are thoroughly secularized.

If God makes no difference, the only source of value is the self.

Types of Relativism

Relativism comes in many shapes and sizes. Some reserve it for a few matters like lifestyle and which style of clothes to wear. Others carry it to great lengths, relativizing everything to the point that, like Nietzsche, they hold that truth is just "a mobile army of metaphors."[5] Nothing is really true as such; all is a matter of social agreement.[6] But what happens when a society agrees to accept a wide variety of "true" but logically contradictory views? In such a situation we have not only the social reality of pluralism (the side-by-side existence of people who hold different worldviews and values) but also the ideology of utter relativism (the value judgment that all values are equally valuable). The university is such a social unit: relativism reigns supreme and anarchy is a constant threat.

In my experience lecturing on campuses both in North America and Europe, I think I can discern at least six distinct ways relativism is expressed. Each deserves to be analyzed separately. The first three will be examined in this chapter, the remaining three in the next.

1. All religions boil down to the same thing.
Our age is an age of religious ignorance. Many modern people have

grown up with very little religious education of any kind. In the United States, religious education in public high schools is systemically avoided; some believe that it is actually illegal. In Britain it is present but given in a watered-down form so that no one of the many religious communities—Jewish, Muslim, Hindu, Buddhist, Christian, Jewish—is offended. Moreover, churches are unsuccessful in educating parishioners beyond very basic matters; sometimes nothing more than vague moral precepts is communicated.

For whatever reason, however, one of the most common forms of relativism is simply based on a fiction: "All religions boil down to the same thing."[7]

But all religions do *not* boil down to the same thing. Many claims of every religion are incompatible with claims of other religions.

Take the notion of fundamental reality. Every religion answers this basic question: *What is prime reality? That is, what is now, always was and always will be?* For Christians, Jews and Muslims the answer is the infinite-personal God who for his own good purposes created the universe. Hindus say it is the impersonal God (Brahman) from whom all transient reality emanates. Zen Buddhists do not believe in God at all but point to the Void, a fundamental indeterminate reality (a nothing-in-particular, neither personal or impersonal) undergirding all transient reality.

From each of these basic commitments come very different religions, each with its own center of meaning, rituals and ethical teachings. There is considerable overlap in ethics and in some practices, but there is no common center.

All one needs to do to see the contradictions between religions is examine what they teach. As we will see below, in answer to "What happens to a person after death?" Christians teach resurrection, Hindus reincarnation and naturalists extinction. What each teaches is a simple matter of information. Moreover, these differences are an essential part of the teachings of these religions. To remove the differences or marginalize them is to deny the religion its right to say what is most important according to its teachings.

Still, many people continue to think that all religions boil down to the same thing. One religion, Baha'i, actually teaches this. And in the recent past, Arnold Toynbee argued that we should develop a single religion, selecting the best insights of each of the major world faiths.

As I write this, the late Joseph Campbell remains popular as an exponent of this view. In his book and television series with Bill Moyers, *The Power of Myth*, Campbell argued that all of the world's myths (with one major exception) tell much the same story, presume much the same notion of fundamental reality and differ (albeit widely) only in details. The main presupposition of all myth is this: the fundamental unity of all reality. That is, the world is an emanation from God (there has been no creation); human beings are essentially divine (they are not made in the image of God; they are God); through ignorance and forgetfulness people are alienated from their source (there has been no Fall in Eden; there is no such thing as sin); salvation is accomplished through grasping who we really are as divine beings (no redemption is needed). Campbell summarizes "myth's one great story" this way: "That we have come forth from the one ground of being as manifestations in the field of time. The field of time is a kind of shadow play over a timeless ground."[8] Then he takes this basic mythic pattern and interprets it under the categories suggested to him by psychologist C. G. Jung, reducing both religion and myth to psychology. The myths tell the psychological truth about human beings in the world.[9]

But Campbell himself admits that the Christian notions of creation, Fall and redemption will not fit this pattern: "Once you reject the idea of the Fall in the Garden, man is not cut off from his source."[10] And Campbell does reject the notion of the Fall. So even the most popular exponent of the notion that all myths—all religions—are basically one has to make a very major concession. Christianity cannot be reduced to the form of his master myth. But that may not be a problem, for, as Robert Segal says, "Throughout his writings Campbell contends that traditional Western mythology, by which he means that of the Bible rather than that of Greece and Rome, is dead."[11] If that is so, then it still might be possible to say all "live" religions are basically the same. But the Christian faith is very much alive, not least in places like Africa where the myths of the primal religions are also most alive.

The upshot is that those who would try to justify their notion that all religions boil down to the same thing, or that the essence of every religion is the same, will not get much useful support from Joseph Campbell. The facts are just too plain: All religions *don't* boil down to the same thing.

2. It's true for you, it's not true for me.
The most common expression of relativism is this: "It's true for you but it's not true for me."

This is of course quite appropriate for matters of taste. Take the following sentences:
- "Strawberry ice cream tastes good."
- "He's a hunk."
- "She's gorgeous."
- "That's a great shirt."

The first sentence, for instance, is certainly true for me. But it just as certainly need not be true for anyone else. It is, of course, true for many people, but it needn't be. Our preference in clothes, music and food is to a large extent governed by taste. Of course, one can argue, and many do, that aesthetic value—the beauty of music, for example—can be shown to have a large measure of objective criteria associated with personal taste. But it is no offense against reason for one person to say "Dizzy Gillespie's jazz is the greatest" and another to say "No; it's really not up to the standard of Thelonius Monk." Both from their personal points of view can be true.

In short, "It's true for you but not for me" is appropriate for *person-specific statements*. It is not, however, appropriate for objective-specific statements. Take the following statements.

☐ "After death each person will eventually be resurrected either to life with God and his people (heaven) or to an existence apart from God (hell)."

☐ "After death the body decays but the soul is eventually reincarnated in another body to become another person."

☐ "After death each person becomes extinct."

At Washington and Lee University I spoke with four students who claimed that all these sentences could be true. A person's belief in resurrection, reincarnation or extinction made it true for each person. That is, those who believe in resurrection will be resurrected; those who believe in reincarnation will be reincarnated; and those who believe in extinction will become extinct at death. The notion seemed so odd that it took several minutes of dialogue before I understood that this was what they were actually claiming.

To see why this kind of relativism cannot be true, consider the consequences if it were. First, it would mean that each person controls ultimate reality simply by believing. It is tantamount to making each person a god—at least a god over his or her own destiny. There is no reason to think human beings have any such power over the forces that govern their deaths.

Still, some students seem to believe that they do have the power to make the world a meaningful place in which to live. Several students, for example, have responded in surveys to the question "Why should anyone believe in anything at all?" by saying this: "If I didn't believe, I (or anything else) would not exist." Indeed, the implicit notion that "believing makes it so" undergirds much relativism in the modern world.

Second, if all three sentences were true, it would mean that ultimate reality is fundamentally incoherent. Resurrection as it is understood in Christian terms is tied in with the notion of a God who created us and in Jesus Christ redeemed us. Resurrection occurs by the power and will of God, not of us. Moreover, in Christianity resurrection is the guarantee that each of us is created in the image of God and each of us has individual dignity. I remain me, you remain you, after death as well as before. We do not become someone else. That makes each of us responsible for our own actions.

Reincarnation as it is understood in Eastern religions is linked with the notion that individuals are not important; they are expendable and do not have any existence beyond their bodily life; what is permanent is the "soul," and that is not tied to any specific individual form.

Extinction requires a universe that has only a material component. When the material that makes up any given person becomes sufficiently disorganized (dies), nothing is left over; the person disappears.

In other words, these ideas—resurrection, reincarnation, extinction—are tied to very complex conceptions of the universe. If one of them is true, the others cannot be true. Logically, all of them could be false and some other view could be true; but if one *is* true, the others are not.

Finally, the view that the universe is incoherent is incompatible with scientific study. If all of three views were true, normal science would not give us uniform results. But our science gives us uniform results. Therefore, the three views of what happens at death cannot all be true, not true even in the sense that each could be true for different sets of people.

3. All religious systems, if followed sincerely, lead to the same spiritual reality. I was once in a public dialogue with a professor of mathematics education. The topic was "Spirituality: New Age or Christian?" The professor defended a New Age position. In his opening statement he announced that he considered all of the following religious texts inspired: the Bible, the Qur'an, the Hindu scriptures and even some messages that come through twentieth-century channelers. He was asked by both the audience and me how he could find all of these texts inspired.

"Each religious text is like a tube down which one looks," he replied. "At the end of the tube is the same spiritual reality."

He was not at all concerned with contradictions between the texts. He had no particular recommendations as to which "tube" one should choose to look down. His only advice was to choose one and follow it to the end.

This claim does not so much say that all religions are the same as that the differences are not finally significant. That is, the claims of one religion do not preclude the validity of the claims of another, even contradictory, religion. It means that the notion of exclusivity itself—a claim made by several religions—cannot be taken seriously.

True, Buddhism and Hinduism do not generally claim exclusivity. Zen teachers will often say that you do not have to abandon your Christian faith to pursue a Zen path. Hinduism often tries to absorb Christianity by saying that Jesus is one of the many avatars (incarnations) of the gods; Christians can be the "Hindus of the West."[12]

In the West one of the early proponents of this view was Sri Ramakrishna, an Indian teacher whose philosophy began to penetrate Western consciousness in the late nineteenth century:

God has made different religions to suit different aspirants, times, and countries. All doctrines are only so many paths; but a path is by no means God Himself. Indeed, one can reach God if one follows any of the paths with whole hearted devotion. . . . As one and the same material, water, is called by different names by different peoples, one calling it water, another eau, a third aqua, and another pani, so the one Everlasting-Intelligent-Bliss is invoked by some as God, by some as Allah, by some as Jehovah, and by others as Brahman. . . . The devotee who has seen God in one aspect only knows him in that aspect alone. But he who has seen him in manifold aspects is alone in a position to say, "All these forms are of one God and God is multiform." He is formless and with form, and many are his forms which no one knows.[13]

We have already seen from the above discussion that each religion sees different things at the end of its "tube." Christians see a personal encounter with a personal God and an existence forever with or without God; Hindus and New Agers see a future of reincarnations until there has been a realization of their own divinity and a reabsorption into the divine essence; Zen Buddhists look toward a grasping of the essence of their existence in the Void.

The only way each of these could be the same final "spiritual reality" is if this "spiritual reality" were totally indeterminate. There are some who think that this is indeed the case.

But Christianity and the other religions of the Book (Judaism and Islam) proclaim themselves as exclusive. Each insists that its teachings, if true, are exclusively (though not necessarily exhaustively) true. That has to be the case, for each of these religions of the Book accepts the notion that utterly contradictory doctrines cannot both be true, and each of these religions has doctrines that contradict those of the other religions, including other religions of the Book.

For instance, Christians insist that Jesus Christ is the Second Person of the Trinity, fully God and fully human. Muslims and Orthodox Jews both reject this, holding the strict monotheistic view that God alone is God. Orthodox Jews and Christians accept a personal God with some characteristics—intimate personal love, for example—significantly different from the Islamic concept of God. All of them proclaim that they alone are the true way.

Notice the claim to exclusivity in Jesus' words: "I am the way and the truth and the life. No one comes to the Father except through me" (Jn 14:6). The apostle Peter is just as clear: "Salvation is found in no one else, for there is no other name under heaven given to men by which we must be saved" (Acts 4:12).

Both Orthodox Judaism and Christianity likewise hold to the exclusivity of the God of the Hebrew Scriptures. Listen to God speaking in Isaiah:

I am the LORD, and there is no other;
    apart from me there is no God.

I will strengthen you,
  though you have not acknowledged me,
so that from the rising of the sun
  to the place of its setting
men may know there is none besides me.
I am the LORD, and there is no other. (Is 45:5-6)

Islam's one creed majors on exclusivity: "There is no God but Allah, and Muhammad is his prophet."

Certainly the history of the people of the Book bears out one grim result of the doctrine of exclusivity: Muslims, Jews and Christians have gone to war for the differences among them. This is not to say that any of these religious groups *should* have taken their differences to these ends; religious war seems especially questionable for Christians, given the teachings of Jesus. But my point here is that all three of these religious groups agree that their central beliefs are essentially true *to the exclusion of those that clearly contradict these beliefs*.

In short, a relativism that proclaims that the "end" of all religions is the same is self-stultifying and self-contradictory. Exclusive claims cannot be negated or reduced to nonexclusive claims without violating the basic rule of relativism itself, which allows all claims to be equally valid.

There is, however, one way out of this trap. That is to say that the final "spiritual reality" is totally indeterminate. There are some who do just that.

Theologian Wilfred Cantwell Smith holds that all worship is valid, "since the reality to which it is directed is unknowable."[14] Smith quotes as "one of the most discerning remarks that I know" the words of the Yogavasistha: "Thou art formless. Thy only form is our knowledge of Thee."[15] Tom Driver makes the same point as Smith: "God has different 'natures.' In pluralist perspective, it is not simply that God has one nature variously and inadequately expressed by different religious traditions. It is that there are real and genuine differences within the Godhead itself, owing to the manifold involvement that God has undertaken with the great variety of human communities."[16]

In both Smith's and Driver's views, God is not to be limited by the law of noncontradiction. He is so indeterminate in form as to be able to appear both personal and impersonal; he is and is not whatever human beings know of him. In his own transcendent essence he is unknowable.

This view has three inherent devastating flaws. First, it requires those who hold the view to know something that the view itself precludes them from holding. If God is unknowable, how can it be known that he or she or it is unknowable? Why should we believe anyone who says this?

If God were determinate enough to be personal and interested in revealing himself to us, he might well tell us that we are unable to know him exhaustively. The God of the Bible does indeed do that:

"For my thoughts are not your thoughts,

neither are your ways my ways," declares the LORD.

"As the heavens are higher than the earth,

so are my ways higher than your ways

and my thoughts than your thoughts." (Is 55:8-9)

But unless we are told by someone who knows, we cannot know what we cannot know. There is no reason to believe Smith and Driver.

Second, the view of God as formless gives no center at all to our religion or philosophy. If final reality is formless, everything is permitted. Such a view makes ultimate reality indeterminate and unknowable. If God or ultimate reality is indeterminate, then there is no final foundation on which to rest our distinctions between good and evil, truth and falsity, honor and dishonor. We have no basis for restraining anyone from doing any action at all—not just from walking on the grass but from beating a little child or raping a college student walking home from a night class. It is the same as if God were dead, for he *is* dead as far as providing humanity with any standard by which to live.

Third, in the words of Lesslie Newbigin, "If ultimate reality is such that he, she, or it behaves in mutually incoherent ways, what possible hope is there for human unity? The corollary of this intellectual collapse is the abandonment of hope for humanity."[17]

Why Relativism?

Why is the atmosphere of relativism so pervasive today? We have already seen that it is fueled at least in part by the "death of God" in our culture. The self alone is left to determine values.

But there is a social reason as well. When people determine their own values without recourse to an objective standard, social chaos is just around the corner. We know—because we have seen this in even the little bit of history we've experienced—that when people disagree on matters so fundamental as sexual ethics and religious doctrine, violent conflict is always a danger. So why don't we just agree to live and let live? Let's agree not only to disagree agreeably; let us remove the disagreement entirely by saying to each other, "Hey, it's okay. It's true for you. It's not true for me, and it doesn't have to be. Let's at least agree that peace and freedom are the prime values to be preserved. You and I are free to believe as we want, but we must not fight over any differences that emerge from exercising our freedom."

But relativism cannot provide a foundation for unity on the basis of freedom and peace. Freedom allows me to believe that I can choose my values, and I can choose to believe that these values are universal, not just limited to me. That means that I am free to believe that you should believe just like me and that if you don't I am free to try to force you to do so. Peace is not compatible with such radical freedom.

If we want to preserve peace, we will have to search elsewhere than relativism for a justification of the value of either peace or freedom.

6
CLOSING A MIND SO OPEN
THAT EVERYTHING FALLS OUT

We believe that truth will only be found
in the next box we open.
When we open that box,
we believe that truth will only be found
in the next box we open.
We believe in a mind so open that everything falls out.
(J. W. SIRE, "CREED II")

F or the time being let's leave Chris, Bill and Bob to their contin-
uing ruminations. Their investigation into relativism does not
run the exact course plotted here. Investigating intellectual
and social forces that are as pervasive as relativism is always a long
process. Clarity and organization of one's conclusions may in fact
never come, or at least not come for months or years. That's why Chris
and Bob, though they do not yet realize this, are on a long quest
whose goal is still only on the horizon. In chapter seven we will return
to them and see how they are getting along.

Relativism comes in many forms. We examined three of them in the
previous chapter. Here we look at three more. The first has some merit,
if accepted in a limited form. The other two are predicated on presuppositions that are at odds with Christian faith, since they are based on
a prior commitment either to radical skepticism or to atheism.

There is, however, a sound reason Christians can be confident that at least limited human knowledge is not only theoretically possible but practically accessible.

4. No religious or intellectual commitments can claim to be true; all are subject to revision.

There is a partial truth in this statement if it is taken in a "soft" form. That is, it is clear that we finite human beings do not have a lock on the way the world is put together. Our systems—whether common-sense or philosophical or theological—are always subject to revision. Tennyson said it well:

Our little systems have their day.

They have their day and cease to be.

They are but broken lights of Thee,

And Thou, O Lord, are more than they.[1]

We would be much better off as human beings if we followed this counsel: "Keep an open mind on all your commitments so that you are always open to correction." But we also need the courage of our convictions. That means we must hold our commitments without any reservation that would keep us from fulfilling to the nth degree what we set our sights toward doing.

But the popular relativism that states, "No religious commitments can claim to be true; all are subject to revision at all times," means something other than this. Taken in its "hard" form it is radical skepticism—the denial that we can know anything at all with any assurance that we are right. Truth escapes us, because we are simply unable to justify our claims to truth.

Stated in its hard form this position is self-contradictory. If everything is subject to revision, so is the statement itself. Hard skepticism (nihilism) claims too much. One can know *that one does not know,* but one cannot know *that one cannot know.*

Skeptics who wish to remain merely skeptics should claim only that they *do not know* and should leave open the possibility that they *can know.* Otherwise they become utter nihilists, and nihilism (because it claims that nothing can be known) is self-referentially incoherent.[2]

The assumption of traditional epistemology, on the other hand, is that our knowledge approaches the truth of various matters, and some of the things we think and believe are closer to the way things are than others. Claims to truth can be justified by past and present experience of oneself and others, by logical internal consistency and by conformity to what has been revealed in authoritative texts—whether those of science or those of religion. Of course, one's belief in those texts themselves can be justified by how well what they say passes the test of reason and experience. That does not mean that either reason or experience is the final arbiter of truth. For Christians the final arbiter is God alone. But it does mean that one can justify one's belief that God is the final arbiter of truth by appeal to reason and experience. It is not unreasonable, for example, to believe that the Bible is the revelation of a holy God to a sinful people.

Lesslie Newbigin has put it this way:

The faith is held with universal intent. It is held not as "my personal opinion," but as the truth which is true for all. It must therefore be publicly affirmed, and opened to public interrogation and debate. Specifically, as the command of Jesus tells us, it is to be made known to all the nations, to all human communities of whatever race or creed or culture. It is public truth. We commend it to all people in the hope that, by the witness of the Holy Spirit in the hearts of others, it will come to be seen by them for themselves as the truth.[3]

If we hold our faith with "universal intent," we will be acknowledging both our own fallibility and our faith in a God who wants us to know the truth. It is a delicate balance—supreme confidence in God's ability to speak clearly versus our own propensity to see things only as we wish to see them, or only as we always have, or only as we do without thinking. But this is the position we are in as Christians—fallen people, redeemed but not yet perfected in glory.

5. All claims of all kinds are claims within a structure of language. They get their truth from their conformity to this structure and the presuppositions that inform it.

This is a difficult concept to understand, because it is counterintuitive. In Western culture we generally assume that we are seeing and talking about what's really there. In order to believe that we are not doing this, we have to think hard and long, usually at the instigation of some sage or philosopher like Chuang Chou or Descartes. So this form of relativism is so far largely confined to the world of academic philosophy, sociology and the humanities. I will present only one form of it here, the form it takes in the philosophy of Richard Rorty.

Essentially, this sort of relativism rejects any notion that there are any knowable essences in reality. It holds that there is nothing essential in the world outside ourselves that we access by either our rational mind or our senses. Our senses apprehend phenomena, but these phenomena do not transmit to us the essences of the objects we are apprehending. Moreover, these phenomena themselves are not solid categories. What we call a tree is different for each of us, because *tree* is a label for phenomena that are multiple and always in flux. Names are as insubstantial as phenomena.

Yet we human beings form languages that give us practical access to each other and the power to control our external environment.[4] Indeed, we form lots of languages. Some of these—like French, English and Swahili—divide us from each other nationally or ethnically. Some—like the language of physics and chemistry—apply to matters of what we call the physical world. Others apply to ethical concerns, still others to religious matters, those discourses in which we talk about the ultimate—God, spirit, divinity, soul, eternal life.

As Charles Taylor, a strong critic of Rorty, says, "Rorty offers a great leap into non-realism: where there have hitherto been thought to be facts- or truths-of-the-matter, there turn out to be only rival languages, between which we end up plumping, if we do, because in some way one works better for us than the others.[5]

Each language is largely self-contained, and there is no way to choose rationally between them, for each has its own rationality, its own way of adjudicating claims to truth. Truth becomes what "works" to get what is wanted. If the locution "Please open the window" gets you what you want, then it has served its purpose. If the Lord's Prayer performs a function that people want, then it, along with the world-view it presupposes, is "true." That there really is a God who is "Father" and who is being "hallowed" by the sincere performance of this prayer is neither true nor false in any shape that can be determined outside the language system—the language of Christian devotion.[6]

The same is true of the Hindu notion that "Atman is Brahman." That is a notion that when set in the matrix of the language system of Hinduism is as unimpeachable as "Hear O Israel: the LORD our God, the LORD is one" (Deut 6:4) set in the language system of Judaism or Christianity. Both languages give shape to phenomena; neither puts us in touch in any sense with anything behind the language itself. Both languages are human products; they are not forced on us by any substantial or transcendent essence.

It is in such a context that we can understand Richard Rorty: "The world does not speak. Only we do. The world can, once we have programmed ourselves with a language, cause us to hold beliefs. But it cannot propose a language for us to speak. Only other human beings can do that. . . . *[L]anguages* are made rather than found, and . . . truth is a property of linguistic entities, of sentences."[7] Truth thus becomes in Nietzsche's phrase "a mobile army of metaphors."[8] Even science has no special status; it is merely "one genre of literature—or, put the other way around, literature and the arts are inquiries, on the same footing as scientific inquiries." Ethics is "neither more 'relative' or 'subjective' than scientific theory."[9]

It is easy to see how this notion, when applied to religious claims or claims to value of any kind, sparks a radical relativism. It is not that all religions lead to the same end—the view we discussed above. It is that each religion makes its own claims in its own language. It can succeed in gaining converts only by making those claims in such a way that it convinces other people to speak the same language. Objective truth has nothing to do with it. Objective truth is inaccessible. In the words of Jean-Paul Sartre, "Given that men are free and that tomorrow they will freely decide what man will be, I can not be sure that, after my death, fellow-fighters will carry on my work to bring it to maximum perfection. Tomorrow, after my death, some men may decide to set up Fascism, and the others be cowardly and muddled enough to let them do it. Fascism will then be the human reality, so much the worse for us. Actually, things will be as man will have decided they are to be."[10]

Rorty quotes the above passage and then comments: "This hard saying brings out what ties Dewey and Foucault, James and Nietzsche, together—the sense that there is nothing deep down inside us except what we have put there ourselves, no criterion that we have not created in the course of creating a practice, no standard of rationality that is not an appeal to such a criterion, no rigorous argumentation that is not obedience to our own conventions."[11] And our own conventions are merely what we have done in the past; they are as malleable as the strength of our ability to get others to agree with us. A Rorty statement I quoted earlier is apropos here again: "A liberal society is one which is content to call 'true' (or 'right' or 'just') whatever the outcome of undistorted communication happens to be, whatever view wins in a free and open encounter."[12]

But in an open society like the university campus, there is seldom any single winning viewpoint on any major issue. There is either a constant contention between alternate views or an abandonment of the quest for any agreement at all. Then follows either of two results: a despair in which the quest for truth is abandoned or a rather easy acceptance of "It's true for you, but it's not true for me."

Rorty rejects the notion that he is a relativist. Only a few freshmen, he says, can be tricked into thinking that contradictory opinions are equally good. But it is difficult to know what else to call a person who holds that we should be content to call "true" whatever is accepted by an open society in open conversation.

Even if agreement is reached and a given position thus "justified" as true, we have not solved the problem of relativism. The word *justified* has to be put in quotation marks. There is no universal system of justification, only those that fit within particular language systems.

But if this is so, then the very statement that each language system provides its own system of justification is itself true only in terms of its own language system. We have here a sort of infinite regress that forever seals off one way of talking from another. There is no reason, for example, that anyone not already accommodated to Rorty's language system should agree with him. What he has said is "true" only for those who are already participating with him in a commitment to the human mind's inability to grasp what is really there.

But surely such an account of what language and reality are is itself either true or false, correct or incorrect. Rorty refuses, and consistently so, to argue for the correctness of his view. He says that he is only putting his views out there in the realm of public discourse to be accepted or not, for this is how such views are justified within his overall philosophy.[13] But the truth question cannot be avoided: Is Rorty right? Even Rorty has to ask himself this question.[14]

If reality is actually a substantial affair, if it actually exists apart from but accessible to our minds, then what these sorts of linguistic relativists are saying is simply false. Christians should, I believe, deny the starting point itself.

Relativism based on the notion of language as the prime constituent of accessible reality is based on a prior rejection of Logos—a rejection of the notion that there is a God who is really real and who is characterized by rationality (Logos). If such a God exists, genuine knowledge of all levels of reality is possible to God. If this God has created people in his image, then at least a partial knowledge of reality is theoretically possible for them as well. Why this is so I will develop in the section below on the Logos as a Christian alternative to relativism.

We turn now to the final form that relativism takes, one that is neither mildly skeptical nor nihilistic, neither linguistic nor nonrealist. Its claims are absolute. In fact, the relativism it proclaims is only partial.

6. God does not exist. Naturalism is true. Religious claims are only metaphors that help people live in harmony. Any metaphor is as good as any other if it leads to harmony, for that is the best we can hope for. There is no life after death.

This final form of limited relativism is, it seems to me, the one that undergirds most secular cultural anthropology and most sociology of religion. Sociologists and cultural anthropologists in general approach their study with the notion that God does not exist. What does exist are multiple ways of understanding the world and our place as humans in it. Every society has its own myths, its self-justifications of its patterns of belief and practice. All of these are literally false. But they nonetheless provide the social cohesion that gives people a sense of identity and purpose. As Joseph Campbell says, "You can have a whole mythology for polygamy, a whole mythology for monogamy. Either one's okay. It depends on where you are."[15] The various religions of various tribes, societies and cultures are therefore each true to the culture itself and true for the culture itself.

People who hold this view take a dim view of any attempt to change people's beliefs. All (every individual or society) are entitled to their own views of the universe. We should live and let live. Changing people's minds introduces disharmony into a tribe, a society, a culture.

There is, of course, a serious flaw in this position. First, it is self-contradictory: if it is true that there is no God, then many religions are simply false and it makes no sense to say that they are "true" for the people who believe them. To leave a people living a delusion is not only elitist but cruel as well.

Second, some religions claim to be true to the way things actually are. And, as we saw above, they make claims to being exclusively true.

They will not accede to the notion that God does not exist or that their beliefs are untrue and only serve to bring social cohesion to their society. They may well be evangelistic and refuse any attempt to be relativized and thus marginalized within the greater pluralistic culture. So this form of relativism cannot deal with a religion or society that simply disagrees with its relativistic thesis.

Third, the claims that this form of relativism makes are either true or false in themselves. Such relativism is not itself a metaphor, nor does it view itself this way. Therefore, it cannot simply be one of many options—including its opposite—available to be chosen.

Logos: A Christian Alternative to Relativism

What we need is a mind with a fine enough net to catch truth when it flies by. And we need a reason to believe that we indeed have such a mind. Is there any reason to think so?

In a previous book, *The Discipleship of the Mind,* I have developed a relatively detailed answer to this question.[16] Here I will summarize some of what I said there about the implications of God as Logos (Jn 1:18).

The first notion on which our confidence in human knowledge rests is that God is alive; therefore there is an ultimate ground in being itself. God is really there—infinite, personal, good, omniscient (intelligent), omnipotent, omnipresent.

Second, God is Logos; therefore reason has an ultimate ground. As John writes in the opening verses of his Gospel, "In the beginning was the Word [Logos], and the Word was with God, and the Word was God" (Jn 1:1). If God is Logos (reason, intelligence, wisdom) itself, then at least one personal being knows everything perfectly. That is what John declares is true of God.

Third, the Logos has become flesh: the kingdom of God has come near. That means that the ultimate ground, God himself, is not alien to human beings. That God could become human without contradiction and without alienation from himself is a confirmation that human beings were themselves made in the image of God. It means that perfect wisdom and intelligence can become embodied in human form. Surely this is a major guarantor of confidence in the possibility of human knowledge.

Fourth, the Logos has created the universe, and thus the universe bears the stamp of God's own rationality: "Through him [the Logos] all things were made" (Jn 1:3). This means that everything in the universe has been made by the One who is intelligence and reason himself. Thus in realizing the intentions of the Logos, the world has an objective purposefulness and is capable of being known, first by God and then by those he made in his image.

Fifth, the Logos is the light of human beings: "In him was life, and that life was the light of men" (Jn 1:4). That is, God has enlightened all human beings so that they can know something of God's world and God himself. Moreover, the Logos has spoken directly to us and given us much specific guidance on the nature of God, the world and ourselves, and on ultimate values. This was true both before and after Logos became flesh. God has spoken to us in many ways through the Old Testament prophets and most fully through the teachings and example of Jesus Christ (Heb 1:1-2).

There is, therefore, a basis on which we can build a Christian alternative to the situation we face. We can challenge the open-ended mind of our culture. We can address the easy acceptance of relativism among students and many others today.

We have a basis, therefore, for closing a mind so open that everything falls out. We can respond to the relativists of the world with solid reasons for holding to the notion that a moral reality exists apart from us. We can be both Christians and academics. There is no dichotomy. All truth is God's truth. The purpose of an open mind is to be open to the truth and then to close on it when it is found.

Thinking gets its value from finding the truth and then not moving from it, no matter how enticing the error. We want a mind closed off at one end. When truth enters it should not slip through.

7
THREE'S A
COMPANY

We believe that everything's getting better
despite the evidence to the contrary.
The evidence must be investigated.
You can prove anything with evidence.
(STEVE TURNER, "CREED")

*C*hris Chrisman, Bill Seipel and Bob Wong: this trio soon became a minicommunity. Having come from very different places, they now found themselves in the same place at the same time with with the same questions. Each of them was confused, but oftentimes about different things.

Chris and Bill believed the Bible would have something important to say about what troubled them if they could just figure out where the relevant passages were and what they meant when they found them.

Bob would have nothing of this, but was no longer confident that his own unaided reason could solve all his problems. He had seen that various people whom he considered rational held such different opinions about the basic makeup of the world that all of them couldn't be right, but he couldn't figure out how to choose among them. Each one required some sort of starting point—some sort of presupposition that had to be accepted on faith. The human mind, he realized, is finite; it just can't know anything for certain, not when you set the mind reflecting back on itself. Everything could be doubted, except the doubting itself while one was doubting. But that kind of self-reflection led nowhere.

Bob had once thought it did, but even in high school he and Michael Stone had concluded that Descartes (who first proposed this technique for finding certain knowledge) had made some logical mistakes and that Descartes's proof of the existence of God based on his "I think, therefore I am" foundation was invalid. They had read about Descartes in the work of one of his critics. Bob couldn't remember the critic's name. In any case, he and Michael had been delighted that it confirmed them in the atheism they found so congenial and exhilarating as high-school students.

At first Bob's faith was naive, unreflective and unchallenged. But Professor Comprel's class changed that. Here was an "intelligent" person who did not think much of the laws of logic when it came to matters of the spirit. But Bob, Chris and Bill began to ask what happens when one abandons reason as a tool of thought, or as a significant motivation to believe one thing rather than another. They could only conclude that what one believed might turn out to be unreasonable. Who wants to believe something unreasonable? Not Bob, not even Chris or Bill.

Of course, even if a belief was unreasonable it could still be desirable: emotionally satisfying, energizing, exciting, new, popular among their friends—intellectual or otherwise. That was attractive. But as the three argued with one another, impaling each other on various horns of various dilemmas, they gradually came to accept as best—if not strictly provable—that reason (by which they meant the laws of logic) had to play a major role in their deliberations.

When the three of them got together, as they did after almost every philosophy class, they homed in on their problems, sometimes with the stimulation of Professor Knock's class, sometimes without it. The chief issue they faced was relativism, and while they did not follow the exact route I took in the previous chapter in this book, they did turn relativism back on itself to see if it accounted for what it pretended to.

Professor Knock was helpful because he reinforced Bob's "faith" in reason. Knock was familiar with freshman nihilists who challenged him by saying that they could not see why the laws of logic were true. Sometimes he would simply ignore the puzzlement of the great unwashed generation he was having to introduce to the art of thought. But when he took the challenge seriously, he called his students to prove that the laws of logic were false and then showed that all of their proofs assumed the truth of the position they were trying to refute. One cannot give reasons for rejecting reason without assuming reason in the process of rejection. "Self-stultification" or "self-contradiction," Professor Knock called it: any proposition that if true requires the proposition itself to be false must itself be false.

Here is how he put it. If "A is not not-A" (the second law of thought) is true, then any given thing is that thing and not its opposite.

His illustration was this: Let A = an edible mushroom; then let not-A = an inedible mushroom (a poisonous mushroom). If is "A is not not-A" is true in general, then an edible mushroom is a not a poisonous mushroom. That makes sense.

But if "A is not not-A" is not true, then "A is not-A" is true. That means that anything can be both itself and its opposite. Or, as in the illustration, an edible mushroom is a poisonous mushroom.

Of course, common sense tells us this is untrue. If it were true, all thinking and communication would be meaningless nonsense. In fact, there would be no difference between true and false. And that just can't be the case if we are to trust our minds at all.

Bob, Chris and Bill tried to give this some relevance to their analysis of relativism. This is the way they argued: If God can be both completely impersonal (Hindu view) and personal (Christian view) at the same time, then A can be both A and not-A at the same time. But something can't both be and not be. Hence relativism, at least in this form, is wrong.

But deciding that relativism is wrong did not solve all their problems. For one thing it did not help them decide between Bob's atheism and Chris and Bill's Christianity. There were endless conversations about that. Bob found himself defending himself not just against Bill and Chris but against his roommate as well, for Bob had come to find in Kevin Leaver a good friend as well as roommate. He and Kevin did not have the same intellectual interests; Kevin just quietly proclaimed his faith in Jesus and urged Bob to read the Bible. It wasn't that Kevin was unintelligent. Quite the contrary. It was just that Kevin was unshaken in his confidence that the Bible told the truth about God and the world. Bob knew that Kevin and his other two friends would like each other if they ever met, but he was almost afraid of what the combination might mean to his ability to hold his own proatheist position. So for several weeks he kept the knowledge of Kevin's existence to himself.

Meanwhile, Chris, Bill and Bob went in quest of something they found they could agree on—the reason or reasons that relativism was so characteristic of the university mind.

Relativism, they concluded, was based on the notion that each person has the authority to decide what is true. Their World Civ text had used a phrase that captured it well, they thought: "the autonomy of human reason." This phrase was used in connection with the Enlightenment, the period of Western intellectual history beginning in the late seventeenth century. It immediately rang a bell with Bill when he first saw it.

When he told the others, Chris could hardly wait to take the ball and run with it. "Yes," he said, "but it's not just a general autonomy belonging to generic humanity. It should be 'the autonomy of *each individual's* reason.' Every person gets to decide what's true. That's why we keep hearing our friends say, 'It's true for you, but it's not true for me.' It's *individualism* that's at the heart of relativism."

Then Chris had another sudden revelation: *individualism* was one of the terms he had been introduced to in Introduction to Sociology.

That course had not meant much to him as he took it, but here was a connection to life. He wished now he hadn't sold his text at the end of the first semester. At least he had his class notes, and they included just what he was looking for—a brief description of individualism as a force of modernity and a reference to the book his professor said was indispensable on this topic: Robert Bellah et al.'s *Habits of the Heart*. Chris remembered seeing a stack of used copies in the bookstore, and he bought one. Its length was a little overwhelming, but Chris had learned to scan-read and in a couple of hours he had identified the chapters that seemed the most relevant. These he read with great attention—and the loss of lots of sleep. This book kept him awake at night.[1]

8
ONE'S
ENOUGH

We believe that each man must find the truth
that is right for him.
Reality will adapt accordingly.
The universe will readjust. History will alter.
We believe there is no absolute truth
excepting the truth that there is no truth.
(STEVE TURNER, "CREED")

What Chris Chrisman found as he read Robert Bellah's *Habits of the Heart* was an analysis of the American mind that went a long way toward explaining what he, Bob Wong and Bill Seipel were feeling.

As Chris passed on what he was learning, the three began to grasp what had been happening to them over the past few months. What, then, is individualism, and why has it proven such a powerful social force?

Individualism Defined

Basically, individualism is a social force, an implicit attitude that permeates the fabric of society. Whether we in the West (especially in North America) know it or not, we act as if each of us were entirely on our own, as if each of us were solely in control of our destiny.

When we find we are not we become upset, disoriented, confused, troubled—and if we are troubled enough we look for a way out, a way back to feeling that we are in control of our own lives.

Individualism proclaims, "I am self-sufficient," "I am who I am," or "I am who I make myself to be." Long before any of us ever heard Frank Sinatra sing them, ringing in our hearts and the foundations of our minds and wills were the words "I gotta be me" and "I did it my way." From high-school English on these lines have rung in my ears:

I am the master of my fate;

I am the captain of my soul.[1]

Such ideas are a part of the cultural heritage of the modern American psyche. They are, of course, lies. But that doesn't keep them from being powerful molders of the modern soul.

Robert Bellah distinguishes between four types of individualism. The first, *ontological individualism,* is generic: the other three are subspecies.

Ontological individualism (a concept introduced by John Locke in the seventeenth century) is the basic notion. "The individual is prior to society, which comes into existence only through the voluntary contract of individuals trying to maximize their own self-interest."[2] The idea is that each person is fundamentally alone. The ego boundaries end with the skin. I am I. You are you. We are a collection of individuals. We are a group, a society, a culture only so long as we agree to be one. Society is not of our essence; it is what we choose to make it.

Locke did not go so far as to say that each person is in control of who he or she is, but he turned the path of psychic history in this direction. Nor did he see that ontological individualism decays into nihilism. As a person takes total control over all reality and becomes the judge and jury for all others, the notion of a norm by which that person is judged disappears. As philosopher Hans Jonas says, "If the good is a mere creature of the will, it lacks the power to bind the will."[3] Thus nihilism. But these are later developments.

In any case, ontological individualism is the basis for republican, utilitarian and expressive individualism.

Republican individualism is epitomized by Thomas Jefferson. Here each individual acts rationally for the interests of others, the larger social whole, because it maximizes one's own freedom and benefit. When many individuals internalize such a notion, a democratic state can be built. A sense of justice and the rights of others teeters on the good will and intention of individuals who see their self-interest supported by good citizenship, but at least there is something on which the formation of a just society can rest.

Much of what I recall being taught about citizenship as a schoolboy rests on this notion. You should be a good citizen because it is really the best thing for you. It's the Boy Scout model.

Utilitarian individualism has its champion in Ben Franklin. Here each individual is seen to have the opportunity to get ahead on his or her own initiative. It produces "a society where each vigorously pursue[s] his own interest."[4] This view "has an affinity to a basically economic understanding of human existence."[5] Success is measured by material acquisitions, social power and prestige.

Utilitarian individualism fuels the engine of Western economy. Horatio Alger, one of the heroes of my generation, wrote stories of office boys (never girls) who rose to be bank presidents and "captains of industry." Lee Iacocca takes on this mythic role today. Here is the individual who single-handedly saves a giant company—all its employees and all its stockholders. Never mind that he drew on the national treasury to do so. He was the ingenious financial engineer who pulled it off. So goes the myth.

Expressive individualism, however, has come to be the dominant form individualism takes today. The essence of expressive individualism is the notion that each individual is free to "cultivate and express the self and explore its vast social and cosmic identities."[6] One is considered "free to express oneself, against all constraints and conventions."[7]

Historically, Ralph Waldo Emerson with his famous essay "Self-Reliance" and Walt Whitman with his once-popular poetry may have set the stage, but the current individualistic hedonism of Hollywood and the energetic search for self-fulfillment and self-expression are the inevitable end of expressive individualism (or at least its current form of expression). One ought not run off to Japan and put oneself under the tutelage of a guru, said the late Joseph Campbell, scholar of mythology and popular pundit. "Our spirituality is of the individual quest, individual realization—authenticity in your life out of your own center. So you must take the message from the East, assimilate it to your own dimension and to your own thrust of life, and not get pulled off the track."[8]

Many in the New Age movement take expressive individualism even further by saying that each of us is divine, the creator not just of our own meanings but of our own destinies as well.[9] Shirley MacLaine proclaims that she created the evening news, the Beatles, chocolate-chip cookies and the Statue of Liberty.[10] In such circumstances the self creates its own moral values. Whatever one wants is okay. Everything is permitted, because there is no one with authority to prohibit. Individualism becomes apotheosis; each person becomes God.

East and West
Before we look at the historical roots of Western individualism, let's take a look at it in light of its opposite—let's call it *communalism*—in the East.

In the West each person is seen as unique and alone. The ego boundaries are firm and end with the skin. Society is just whatever the individuals who make it up decide that it will be. Associations are voluntary. In America most people belong to a dozen different groups and think no more of joining them and leaving them than of throwing away one well-used pair of shoes for a new pair.

In the East, who any given individual is depends on who he or she is in community. The ego boundaries are indeterminate and blend into the ego boundaries of others, first within one's own family and then within the larger surrounding clan and society. It is the family, the clan, the society, whose boundaries are firm; they remain regardless of who the individuals are within the group.

One of the best illustrations of the social effect of these differences is engagement and marriage. In the West, only two people have to agree in order to get married. Of course, most couples want to involve many more in the celebration, but not in the choice. In the East, marriages traditionally are arranged by families after much consideration and bartering.

Where the difference becomes problematic is when American-raised Asians want to marry someone who has not, and perhaps never will, receive the approval of parents and the extended family. The tension is not just between the children and their parents, but within the children themselves. Their own sense of who they are and what they ought to do is at stake; they feel the pull of both cultures.

If Bob Wong ever "falls in love" and decides to marry without his parents' consent, he will feel this tension in a direct and personal way. Bob is as American as he can possibly be, given his past, but he is not so Western that nothing of the East is left to tug at his soul.

We don't have to go as far east as China or Japan to see the remarkable difference between American individualism and its counterpart in other countries. Anthony Ugolnik, in a brilliant comparison of Russian and American mindsets, notes the way this difference is played out in hockey. "The Russians feature precision, in-concert teamwork, skating with blades flashing in synchrony on the ice, while the Americans try to set up scenarios within which an individual player, darting out into an opportunity, can flash forth to a goal."[11] He quotes a Russian woman's comments to a group of his American students: "You are such individualists . . . as if alone you could decide everything. We instinctively seek to express the mind of the community to which we belong."[12] Ugolnik summarizes: "For the Russian Christian, consciousness is a communal product. The self is not owned; it is the product of interaction."[13]

This cultural difference is played out not just in secular terms but in religious ones as well. Moreover, there is not just a contrast between the Eastern religions of Hinduism and Buddhism and the Western religions of the Book (Judaism, Christianity and Islam). There is a difference in how Western religions are practiced in the East. Eastern Orthodoxy, for example, preserves more of the corporate character of Judaism and first-century Christianity than either Catholicism or Protestantism does. This may, in fact, make it more biblical to that extent.

Historical Roots of Individualism

Western individualism ultimately has its roots in the Judeo-Christian concept of human nature. This we will see in chapter ten. But the peculiar form individualism has taken in Northern Europe and North America can be traced to the Renaissance and the Reformation. In the Renaissance of the sixteenth century in Europe, greatly increased attention was given to human beings as such. No longer did artists paint Jesus with a halo; they saw him as a man or as a typical human baby in the arms of a typical human mother. The feet of the apostles rested on the ground. Human reason was given greater scope in theology and biblical studies as scholars gave theologians more accurate Greek texts of the New Testament.

But the key move was made by Martin Luther, not because he sought greater freedom for himself personally, not because he came by individualism through a biblical study of the topic, but because he found that the teachings of the church and the counsel of his spiritual advisers did not satisfy his pursuit of peace with God. Peace with God came when he grasped what Paul in his letter to the Romans meant by "the just shall live by faith" (Rom 3—5). What Luther thought the text meant was different enough from what the contemporary teachers of the church said it meant that he was charged with heresy.

Despite many attempts to reach agreement or compromise by both

Luther and the hierarchy of the church, Luther finally faced a show-down. Luther was told that he must accept the teaching of the church, but he could not do so. Here is what he said to his examiner at the Diet of Worms (April 18, 1521):

> Since Your Majesty and your lordships desire a simple reply, I will answer without horns and without teeth. Unless I am convicted by Scripture and plain reason—I do not accept the authority of popes and councils, for they have contradicted each other—my conscience is captive to the Word of God, I cannot and will not recant anything, for to go against conscience is neither right nor safe. God help me. Amen.[14]

Then he added: "The pope is no judge of matters pertaining to God's word and faith. But the Christian man must examine and judge for himself."

"Here," Roland H. Bainton comments, "we have the epitome and the extent of Protestant individualism."[15] Indeed, here is the "Protestant principle": Each person has both the right and duty to live by his or her own conscience. The conscience cannot be forced.

Notice that Luther did not imply that he was replacing God's authority with his own. He was not affirming the autonomy of human reason. No, quite the opposite. His conscience is "captive to the Word of God." He will believe and act on whatever the Word of God says. The issue is, rather, who is to say what the Word of God means. To whom is given the task of rightly interpreting Scripture? Luther did not complain that only he could interpret Scripture; he was happy to listen to the counsel of others. The problem was, who will take responsibility for making the final decision when interpreters disagree and become deadlocked over their disagreements? Luther said that at that point each individual has to make the determination on his or her own: "The Christian man must judge for himself."

It is nonetheless true that from this point in church history, the church has split and divided, split and divided, hundreds of times. Today's many denominations bear the marks of human divisions along national, racial, ethnic, economic, theological, ecclesiological and intellectual lines. We can point to Luther as the origin of the basic principle on which these divisions occur.

Yet many of us—both Catholic and Protestant—must affirm that, given the circumstances, Luther was right. He had to do what he did. For not only did his action lead to the reformation of many churches and peoples, it triggered a response in the Catholic church to clarify its teachings and purify its church life.

The divisions between Christians now run deep. Many of these divisions are artificial and unbiblical; many are deeply personal and have little to do with doctrine or practice; many are purely geographical or national. A great healing among divided Christians has been taking place in the last forty years, but much more healing is necessary. It is no longer so odd to see Lutherans getting along with Baptists in common projects. And the divide between Catholic and Protestant is being examined with fresh insight and some hope of reconciliation.

But the spirit of individualism has so permeated the fabric of Western society that we are divided not only *between* denominations and congregations but also *within* denominations and congregations. Individuals want to do their own thing, believe whatever they choose regardless of the teaching of their churches. American Catholics are especially loath to accede to the teaching of their church when it disagrees with their desires. The issues of birth control, abortion and priesthood for women are cases in point.

We do not need at this point to give a detailed history of the development of Western individualism. Suffice it to say that it expanded from its Protestant roots as Separatist Puritans left England for the New World and as the frontier mentality sent pioneers westward across the mountains and prairies and the American myth was born ("you can do anything you set your mind to; you can be president of the United States").

The lure of America has been strong. My grandfather Paul Louis Eugene Sire followed his cousin Jules from Switzerland to the United

States in 1891. He sloughed off as much of the Old World as possible as he moved to Nebraska and began to make his way in the New World. Cheated out of his life investment in a herd of cattle, he found himself bankrupt. His eldest son, my father, then dropped out of his first year of college to help keep the family afloat. My dad began to build a new herd of purebred Hereford cattle and made a modest success of ranching. Though my father would work around the house in a farmer's cap, his Sunday-go-to-meetin' clothes were a Western shirt, cowboy boots and a cowboy hat. Even in his eighties, had you given him a horse and a six-shooter he would have ruled the range again.

My heritage is the heritage of American individualism. That's how the West was won. Highly individualistic people who trusted themselves, and sometimes God, moved into a hostile environment and subdued the land, conquered its few Native American inhabitants and built a new society—a society of individuals. My father's hero, though he would probably never say so, was John Wayne. His favorite president was Ronald Reagan. The myth lives on as I too tug against my roots in individualism.

The lure of freedom from oppression has brought many immigrants to the North America. But political freedom in the United States has been tied to individualism, and many became disillusioned. Polish expatriate Czeslaw Milosz describes some of them:

People decided to leave their villages and little towns in the same spirit as man considers suicide; they weighed everything, then went off into the unknown, but once there, they were seized by a despair unlike anything they had ever experienced in the old country. They were accustomed to earning their bread by the sweat of their brow, but their work had been incorporated into the rituals of a community with traditions, beliefs, and the blessings of neighbors. Death as a sanction, "He who doesn't work, doesn't eat," was a part of human fate, accepted in silence, but it was not inflicted on people as individuals—the yoke was borne by everyone together, family, relatives, friends. Now each of them was assessed as an individual, and, isolated among the isolated, they earned their living for a few dollars a day. . . . Then they began to cling to one great dream—to go back. At the same time pride would not allow them to admit their mistake, and they wrote lying letters home reporting that they were doing splendidly.[16]

Still, before we dismiss individualism as a total evil, we should look at the distinct value it has brought to some cultures.

The Values of Individualism

It is extremely important not to reject individualism in toto. It does have a biblical basis, and, properly conceived, it is liberating. Even secular Western individualism has some salutary effects. We will note two that are central to individual dignity and social justice.

First and most important, individualism undergirds respect for all individuals no matter what their ethnic, social, intellectual or economic association. This is especially valuable in a pluralistic society like the United States. If our neighbors next door or in the nearby suburb or city are different from us or from those closest to us in social "status," that makes them no less valuable as persons.

Political scientist Glenn Tinder puts it clearly:

> The Lord of all time and existence has taken a personal interest in every human being, an interest that is compassionate and unwearying. The Christian universe is peopled exclusively with royalty. . . . To speak cautiously, the concept of the exalted individual implies that governments—indeed, all persons who wield power—must treat individuals with care. . . . [Care] always means that human beings are not to be treated like the things we use and discard or just leave lying about.[17]

Tinder further notes: "No one, then, belongs at the bottom, enslaved, irremediably poor, consigned to silence; this is equality. This points to another standard: that no one should be left outside, an alien and a barbarian."[18]

Second, individualism limits the exaltation of social, ethnic, racial, economic or intellectual identification to give status. The tendency of every group is to take for itself the power of giving status to individuals. It leads people to say to themselves, whether consciously or not, "I have dignity *because* I am a Native American, or a Romanian, or a Hungarian, or a person of color or English."

There is certainly a great truth in genuine *multiculturalism*. True multiculturalism as an ideal, and as practiced by many Christians and Christian groups, acknowledges the unique contribution of every culture. It celebrates cultural diversity.

To take pride and pleasure in one's ethnic heritage is both natural and good. For me to look back on my roots in Switzerland, France and England is to know that who I am is very much dependent on who my forebears were. I owe my very existence to this heritage. To try to cut myself off from these roots would be to deny who I am. People do get much of their identity from their families, their immediate societies and the larger culture of which they are a part.

Still, there is a limit to be put on this reflection. The moment it becomes the foundation for my dignity, the reason I have value, it becomes idolatrous. God is the judge over every culture, for each culture represents the machinations of fallen human beings creating for themselves patterns of behavior and belief that are at odds with the will of God and need reformation and redemption.

Moreover, we do not get our value from society, or from our connection to our families or our ethnic roots. We get our value from being made in the image of God for community with each other and ultimately for the glory of God. Western individualism's emphasis on the value of each person has had many good effects.

Recently, however, there has been a resurgence of ethnicism on university campuses. Often in response to overt acts of racial prejudice, students have retreated into supposedly safe enclaves of their own making. Take Oberlin College, once a leader in civil rights and an open society. "Oberlin's student groups undergo a perpetual process akin to what biologists call mitosis. They keep dividing themselves into separate units. Amid charges of racism and sexism, the Lesbian, Gay, and Bisexual Union recently splintered into four narrow factions: Gay Men of Color, Zani (lesbians of color), Lesbians Be Loud (white lesbians), and the Gay Men's Rap Group (gay white men)."[19] At the same time the Asian-American Alliance split into several groups. Residential "program houses," intended to bring together students with like study interests, have become like South African homelands. Students cordon themselves off within these living units, assume a group mentality and cease to operate with the kind of individual freedom that has been historically characteristic of this college.

Ironically, this new mentality is sometimes called "multiculturalism." In this form, however, it is an ideology that proclaims that "race is the determinant of a human being's mind, that the mind cannot, and should not, try to wrest itself from its biological or sociological origins."[20] And further: " 'Multiculturalism' holds that the traditional idea of free thought is an illusion propagated by the spoilers of freedom, by the relations of power that obtain in any given society. It holds, more specifically, that the old liberal notion of freedom is only a sentimental mask of a power structure that is definitionally oppressive of those who are not white Western males.[21]

Such a view is devastating to both individual dignity and social cohesion, especially in a pluralist society. Individualism curbs this tendency. Each person is seen to be valuable for being an individual person, not for being a member of a privileged class.

Ill Effects of Individualism

Western individualism, however, also has a host of ill effects. Those who would look to the West and especially to the United States as a model to emulate should look again.

First, with individualism the values we live by tend to become strictly personal and private. Marriage is okay as long as it fulfills my needs. Sex of all kinds is okay as long as every partner consents and no one is hurt. Whatever I feel right about doing is perfectly satisfactory; after all, who is there to deny me the right of living my life the way I choose?

Second, too few people look at the social consequences of their lifestyle or the actions of their company. The tragic consequences of divorce should be measured in part by the trauma to children. Children who should be raised in a stable family environment are pulled in two or three directions as parents vie for their custody and their affection.

Individuals seeking advancement in their careers ignore the just claims of their supervisees, the just claims of their company to receive the best from them for the company and the just claims of the social and physical environment. Communities are destroyed by managers who place their own advancement over the claims of the community.

Third, religious values are privatized, reined in from making any claims on the social order. As Os Guinness is fond of quoting from Theodore Roszak, Christian faith in a Western individualistic society becomes "socially irrelevant, even if privately engaging."[22]

Fourth, individualism enhances the natural human bent toward selfishness, greed and pettiness. The more we concentrate on our own needs and desires, the more we reap the personal consequences of a warped character.

Finally, individualism leads to loneliness. If we are forever attending only to our own petty wants and wishes, we will be left alone to attend to them all by ourselves. Then we suffer from a loneliness brought on by our selfishness. Worse, we are not likely to know how we became lonely or recognize that the cure is not to continue desperately to try to fulfill our own needs, but simply and quietly to serve others.

Marks of Individualism in the Church Today

We have already noted the connection between individualism and denominational divisions, and individualism's tendency to trigger private theologies and new churches. But even where an individual church or denomination is strong and healthy, individualism has made inroads with regrettable consequences.

Often in these churches, especially those of an evangelical or fundamentalist bent, the gospel becomes oriented only to the individual. "Not my brother, not my sister, but it's me, O Lord, standing in the need of prayer." Salvation is seen solely as individual, and what is saved is called one's "soul." There is a loss of the sense of the whole person, let alone of the sense of community.

In some cases, a "gospel" of self-esteem and self-fulfillment replaces the good news of the kingdom of God. "Christ is the answer" as long as the questions are all personal. Just ask what Christ has to say about some economic problem or some problem larger than the individual—such as whether a nuclear waste dump should be built in the county—and icy stares will come from pastor and people alike.

"The church is okay as long as it fulfills my needs" is the basic attitude of many churchgoers. Americans especially find it easy to move from one church to another, even when they are not moving homes. Ecclesiastical vagabondism rather than long-term or deep commitment—even of Christians to Christians—is the result. Just try to get any individual to become immersed in a long-term project. Pastors, church leaders, leaders of college groups—all find it hard to form lasting communities of Christians who really care for each other.

With so little that Christian leaders can count on from laypeople in the congregation, "I can do it myself" becomes the way of Christian "pros," Christian leaders. Pastors try to become superstars, and a few do, inspiring even more to try.

Roots and Fruit

We Westerners sink our roots deep into individualism. From this soil comes our nourishment. It is no wonder that the fruits of our lives are so dry and tasteless.

We need to be transplanted into soil that is rich in communal nutrients. But does such a field exist? Where do we find it?

9
FOUR'S A COMMUNITY

We believe that man is essentially good.
It's only his behaviour that lets him down.
This is the fault of society.
Society is the fault of conditions.
Conditions are the fault of society.
(STEVE TURNER, "CREED")

*T*he second semester was moving right along. Midterms had come. Chris and his friends had done well. In fact, Chris's English teacher had become quite impressed with his papers. Most of the class was struggling along, writing C-ish and C+ish papers. A few with rhetorical skills were writing B-ish papers. But Chris and a couple of others were constantly in the B-to-full-A range.

Chris was enjoying writing about *Zen and the Art of Motorcycle Maintenance.* Here in one novel were the ruminations of a man who was a lot more confused than Chris and his friends, a lot more emotionally disturbed, but no more concerned to find the truth. While Chris did not understand all the permutations of the narrator's philosophic meanderings—even after his instructor had explained them—still he grasped the essence of the search and actually found it exhilarating to write papers about it.

There was a long section in the book in which the narrator, who had taught English composition at Montana State University, reflected on how he tried to get his students to write for "Quality." One student, try as she would, could think of nothing to write about. The instructor finally told her to write about a single brick in a single building in downtown Boseman. It was the perfect cure, producing a paper that was sheer joy to read.

Chris tried this method on himself, though he did not have her writing block to remove. He wrote a paper about a single dirty spoon he found on an otherwise empty table in the cafeteria. It started as pure description, then shaded gradually into a meditation on the loneliness of the abandoned wretched of the earth, who themselves came to stand for all of humanity.

His instructor loved it. Chris had slipped orthodox Christian theology right past the nose of his philosophy-minded literature-loving English teacher.

His instructor had already come to look forward to Chris's papers surfacing in his biweekly stack of student papers. For Chris was writing about relativism, individualism, the search for truth, and as he wrote he didn't mechanically summarize what he took to be Pirsig's views, but used those views and incidents in the novel to make his own observations. Sometimes he was more tentative than Pirsig, sometimes more certain. But his work was always honest, often insightful and occasionally profound. By the time the class had reached the end of the novel and had to select term-paper topics, Chris was certain of what his would be, if the instructor would allow it.

What he suggested in a one-page proposal was this: "The Theology of *Zen and the Art of Motorcycle Maintenance:* Is Quality God?" His instructor was a bit taken aback by the boldness of Chris's proposal. This was a mighty big topic, but he approved it, and Chris set out to do his first work in theology.

Bill Seipel was also having a good semester. With Chris's help he had settled into life in a secular university and was beginning to get a grip on what had troubled him the first few weeks. His contact with

Bob Wong provided an added stimulation to get his own intellectual house in order. He needed more than ever to *know* what he really believed and why. His weekly Bible studies with Chris on the Gospel of Mark were helping.

More and more, he and Chris were coming to understand who Jesus showed himself to be while he was on earth. More and more it became clear that Jesus was an amazing enigma—a unique blend of the human and the divine. He was a man. No question. But he was also God. He told ordinary stories, but they were exceptionally clever. They not only grabbed your attention, they trapped it and you. Jesus just had to be real, they concluded; his presence leaped from the page. He could not have been invented by anyone.

Bill and Chris prayed together, too. Not long prayers, but prayers expressing honest gratitude for what they were learning in Scripture and in their classes, and prayers for their friends, especially Bob Wong. They had come to admire Bob—his openness to their arguments, his honesty in saying when he could and could not answer their contentions, and his graciousness in accepting them even while he rejected their case for Christianity. And they had learned a lot from Bob, not the least of which was that they didn't know how to answer some of his objections to Christianity. That made them scramble for answers.

Bob, for his part, was more and more in a quandary. There was his roommate's quiet Christian confidence, his philosophy-class partners' friendly attention to his own views, Professor Comprel's fuzzy-minded religiosity, Professor Knock's rock-hard affirmation of the primary role of reason in determining truth, his parents' letters asking him how he was getting along, his own frustration at not being able to convince himself of much of anything.

Bob felt like Chuang Chou, an ancient Chinese philosopher whom Professor Knock had mentioned in one of his rare whimsical moments. Chuang Chou had dreamed he was a butterfly, and when he woke up he wondered whether he was Chuang Chou having dreamt he was a butterfly or a butterfly dreaming he was now Chuang Chòu. Chuang Chou could not get out of his dilemma, nor could Bob Wong.[1]

The fact is that the three young men's study of relativism had left them with a renewed confidence in the use of logic and the value of human reason. But it had not given them a good way to summarize their conclusion. It was then that Bill's study of *The Gospel in a Pluralist Society* paid off. Bill was preparing to write his term paper for Professor Knock when the solution the three were looking for suddenly appeared in the pages of Newbigin's book.

Bill had found that reading Newbigin was like reading precisely what he had already thought or was about to think, only much, much better, much, much clearer. Newbigin confirmed, for example, that "every kind of systematic thought has to begin from some starting point." This starting point has to be taken as "given." His philosophy professor had called this a "presupposition" or a "pretheoretical commitment." In other words, the atheist and the Christian are on the same epistemological grounds; both have to *assume* that something is true before they can *prove* that something else is true. Even a scientist has to assume the truth of two notions: that "the universe is rational and that it is contingent."

Second, Bill learned that the truth of Christianity cannot be confirmed if one accepts as a starting point the same grounds as the atheist. An atheist has to assume a confidence in the finite human mind, a confidence that Christians believe is not justified. Because of the notion of creation and the Fall, a Christian assumes that the human mind is not adequate to find truth on its own. The issue is, then, which assumption is more likely to be true?

After Bill had read some fifty pages of Newbigin, the key idea hit him. Newbigin was discussing the views of Michael Polanyi:

> The scientist who commits himself to the new vision [a change in what had been thought to be true before] does so—as Polanyi puts it—with universal intent. He believes it to be objectively true, and he therefore causes it to be widely published, invites discussion,

and seeks to persuade his fellow scientists that it is a true account of reality. . . . It is his personal belief to which he commits himself and on which he risks his scientific reputation. But at no state is it merely a subjective opinion. It is held "with universal intent"— as being a true account of reality which all people ought to accept and which will prove itself true both by experimental verification and also by opening the way to fresh discovery. It is offered not as private opinion but as public truth.[2]

Universal intent: that was it. One did the best one could with the tools at one's disposal—reason, experience and, for Bill and Chris, revelation. One could take a problem like relativism, consider it from as many angles as one could, and then reach a conclusion that one held with "universal intent." Some matters, like the great conundrum of predestination and free will which had occupied some of Bill's time in high school, might have to be held at a distance. But other matters, like whether Jesus was a worthy teacher to believe and a proper Lord before whom to bow, could not be held at a distance. They demanded decision.

Chris and Bill did not have much doubt about Jesus, of course. They had been Christians long enough to have experienced new life for some time, but they could not prove their view to Bob Wong—or Ralph Imokay, for that matter. Still, they felt that they had good reasons for it and that their view was true. On the other hand, they knew that there was much to know about Jesus which they did not know, and some of this might change their current view of Jesus. But now they could see a way to hold their specific theology (or Christology) both with confidence and with humility. They would be willing to change their mind if that could be justified.

Bob Wong liked this notion as well. It solved the problem of relativism for him too. What he had a hard time accepting is that it came from a Christian theologian. Could any good thing come from there?

But universal intent only gave the three a label for their view of reason and its value. It did not tell them which views they should hold

with universal intent. Should I hold with universal intent the notion
that Jesus is the only way to God? Or should I hold that God does not
exist at all?

All three of them needed some help here.

Up to this point Bob hadn't talked to Chris and Bill about his
roommate, Kevin Leaver. But one day about midsemester, Chris came
across campus to Bob's dorm, and there was Kevin. Since Bob was out,
the two quickly discovered each other to be Christians.

Both were delighted, especially since it meant that Bob had more
than one set of Christian friends. Kevin had seen Bob becoming a bit
more open to hearing about Kevin's faith, and he could now see why.

It was obvious to both Chris and Kevin that, except for their specific
Christian faith and their common interest in seeing Bob become a
Christian, they had very different interests. Kevin was single-mindedly
pursuing a degree in premed and had little interest in anything as
esoteric as philosophy. For him English Comp was a hurdle he was
willing to learn to leap but was unwilling to learn to love, or even like
for that matter. His teacher had chosen Chaim Potok's *The Chosen* as
the novel for the semester, and when Kevin found out that Chris was
reading *Zen and the Art of Motorcycle Maintenance,* his confidence in the
providence of God was reaffirmed. His novel was almost pure story,
not much of that heady stuff.

But Kevin did have two surprises for Chris. First, he was involved
with a whole group of Christians who met every week in Hansom
Union for singing, Christian instruction and fellowship. They called
themselves Hansom Christian Fellowship and were associated with a
national—Kevin thought maybe international—organization whose
name sounded like a college athletic association but really wasn't.
Someone said it had begun in ancient England, maybe even as long
as a century ago, had come to Canada and then had crossed the
border into the U.S. somewhere in the misty midregions of fifty years
ago. Kevin wasn't sure about that, but he was sure that Chris should
get involved.

But the second surprise was bigger. When Chris said where he lived, Kevin said he knew only one Christian who lived in that dorm, a redhead named Susie.

"I thought she was a Mormon," Chris said. "She carries a Book of Mormon with her textbooks!"

"No," Kevin insisted, "she's is a Christian, a very quiet one, but a Christian."

Chris suddenly remembered the vow he had made at Christmastime—to find a female friend and bury himself in a meaningful relationship. But he didn't find himself interested in any of the women he had met in the dorm or in his classes, except for Susie. *How inept at human relations could I be!* he mused.

He vowed never to be so inept again. This time he kept the vow.

Hansom Christian Fellowship had its regular main meetings on Friday night. So Chris and Bill (who was happier to hear about the Fellowship than he was about Susie) attended. It was rather a sacrifice, since both had planned to work on their term papers in philosophy. But Chris wanted to see if Susie was really there, and Bill wanted to broaden his Christian contacts. It was a good move for both of them.

There was singing, praying, information about summer training programs and mission opportunities, a skit promoting a weekend retreat, and a good talk by Maria Marquez. Maria was sort of the "campus pastor" (Chris couldn't think what else to call her) of the Fellowship. Her topic was "Christian Community: A Response to Campus Chaos." Chris and Bill said afterward that the whole evening was like being "slain in the Spirit," not that either of them really understood what that phrase meant to their Pentecostal friends.

The gist of what Maria said we will see in the following chapter. For now we need to know that Chris met Susie for the first time, and it was for both of them infatuation at second sight. Susie could hardly believe Chris was a Christian. She had heard him talk philosophy with the dorm meditators and had assumed he was an intellectual nerd. And as Chris told her, "I thought you were a Mormon. What's with the Book of Mormon you carry to class?"

"What are you talking about? I don't do that."

"Well, don't you remember when I bumped into you, you dropped it and I picked it up and gave it back to you?"

"Oh, that. Good grief. Two young guys in dark suits and narrow ties had just given it to me in the dorm lounge. I haven't even opened the cover!"

Hasty generalization, Chris thought to himself. *Guilt by association,* he muttered under his breath. *Sheer stupidity,* he almost said aloud. *She's probably taken. She could have been mine. I will live my life forever deprived of the only helpmeet God will give me. I should have spoken to her before. I'm lost. I will enter a monastery. No, I'm not a Catholic. I will go to the Bongo Bongos as a missionary. I will tread the burning sands for Jesus.*

"Would you like to go for Coke and ice cream?" Chris was quick to recover.

"Yes," she said simply.

And that was the beginning of a beautiful friendship.

10
COMMUNITY
AMID CHAOS

We believe in getting along with everybody,
so long as there is something in it for us.
Of course if it costs too much to love our neighbor,
well, economics is where it's at, really.
I mean, we can't be responsible for everyone.
(J. W. SIRE, "CREED II")

C hris Chrisman didn't know it yet, but by going to the meeting
of Hansom Christian Fellowship he had found community. He
had already experienced the beginnings of community in his
friendship with Bill Seipel and Bob Wong. Already this friendship was
beginning to make a difference in his attitude to the university. Hansom State no longer seemed so alien—or rather, he was learning to
cope with his alienation by finding fellow aliens.

In Hansom Christian Fellowship he had found a whole bunch of
aliens, and it felt good. It felt good not just because one of those aliens
was Susie, though she was certainly the most interesting alien. Nor did
it feel good solely because he had found an emotional home in a
congenial group. It also felt good because it assured Chris that he and
Bill and Kevin were not the only ones who believed in God—and not
just the Mush God of some of his dormmates, a God one could ma-
nipulate into justifying one's lifestyle, but rather a God of justice as well

as mercy, a God who holds people responsible for their thoughts and deeds.

Chris didn't know this yet, either, but he had found a *plausibility structure* strong enough to confirm and sustain what up to this point had been his private beliefs—held, except for Bill and Kevin, almost entirely in isolation. The concept of *plausibility structure* had been casually referred to in his sociology text the previous semester, but he had not grasped its significance, nor would he become fully aware of the notion for some time yet. But the effect of a congenial plausibility structure was now active in his life, and it was helping Chris without his knowing it.

For Maria Marquez, the staffworker for Hansom Christian Fellowship, the value of community for *plausibility structure* was far from her mind. She was interested in something else. Maria had been feeling rather glum about HCF. Though she had kept her feelings to herself, she had been disappointed in the group this year. Now she had the opportunity to do something about it. She had been asked by the leaders to speak on whatever she felt the group needed.

It didn't take Maria long to make a list for herself, a rather long one. But as she looked at all the items—evangelism, prayer, Bible study, missions—one kept rising to the top of her consciousness. She prayed about it and felt that it indeed was what she should talk on. So Maria plumbed her Bible and her library for what they could tell her about community.

The problems she saw were these: Christian students intent on only their own goals, committees that were not functioning, leaders who took over when committees failed, other leaders who did not even do what they had said they would do, let alone help take up the slack, students who rarely went to church on Sunday because the churches did not "meet their needs." Granted, there were bright spots in the group. The large group meetings were drawing seventy to eighty students week after week, and there were a half-dozen live and functioning small groups. But as a whole, Hansom Christian Fellowship was not a community. It was a bunch of bunches with a bunch of stragglers. As she thought about it, she concluded that HCF was suffering from the disease of Western individualism.

First she thought about launching into a diatribe. "The Lone Ranger Rides Again and Again and Again," she would call her talk. That was the title used by a special speaker she had heard at a staff conference of the national movement she belonged to. It fit him: his hair was gray. But for her students the title was too much from the past. So she considered "Han Solo, Indiana Jones and the Death of Christian Fellowship." Then she realized she was being melodramatic, and, besides, to label disease is not to cure it. Why not go directly to the cure? So she did. She called her talk "Christian Community: A Biblical Perspective." Much of what follows parallels her presentation.

Community: An Old Testament Perspective

The biblical answer to our human longing for meaning and significance is neither archindividualism nor extreme communalism, nor is it a blend—half of one and half of the other. It is rather a third thing: it involves *community*.

The pattern is set at the very beginning of human history. Human beings are made "in the image of God":

God created man in his own image,

in the image of God he created him;

male and female he created them. (Gen 1:27)

From the beginning there is a unity and a diversity, both a oneness and a twoness, to the human frame. Each person is made in the image of God, but the image of God is corporate. No person is alone in the image of God. The very image itself is corporate. Genesis does not elaborate on the corporate character of God, but in the New Testament God is seen to be Father, Son and Holy Spirit, a concept the early church developed into the doctrine of the Trinity.

But here it is already in essence in Genesis itself: human beings as male and female, each and both reflecting the nature of God.

To make this *community* more obvious, the Bible tells the creation story a second time: "The LORD God formed the man from the dust of the ground and breathed into his nostrils the breath of life, and the man became a living being" (Gen 2:7). God then put the man in the Garden of Eden:

The LORD God said, "It is not good for the man to be alone. I will make a helper suitable for him. . . .

So the LORD God caused the man to fall into a deep sleep, and while he was sleeping, he took one of the man's ribs and closed up the place with flesh. Then the LORD God made a woman from the rib he had taken out of the man, and he brought her to the man.

The man said,

"This is now bone of my bones
   and flesh of my flesh;
she shall be called 'woman,'
   for she was taken out of man."

For this reason a man shall leave his father and mother and be united to his wife, and they will become one flesh. (Gen 2:18, 21-24)

In the boldness and beauty of this story, we must not miss the message for us: *it is not good for the man to be alone.* Adam and Eve were a part of each other. Neither Adam nor Eve was meant to stand alone. They were meant to be together. The picture is not just a beautiful glimpse of what marriage is to be; it is a model for human society in general. Adam and Eve were given dominion over the world and were instructed to "fill the earth." A human community was to emerge that would involve, as would Adam and Eve, both the value of the individual and the value of the whole.

Tragically, as the story unfolds in Genesis 3, the serpent tempted Eve. She succumbed to the temptation, and then in corporate solidarity with her Adam succumbed as well. The whole human race fell into alienation from and rebellion against God. So, as Adam and Eve represent the solidarity of the human race in creation, they also represent the solidarity of the human race in their fallenness and need for redemption.

Throughout the Old Testament, the corporate nature of humanity is emphasized. "I will walk among you and be your God, and you will be my people," God says (Lev 26:12). God's plan for the redemption of humanity combines the individual and the corporate at every turn. God saves one man, Noah, and his family from the destruction of the flood (Gen 6—9) and replenishes the earth by his progeny. He calls one man, Abraham, out of Ur of the Chaldees to form the Hebrew people, by whom all the families of the earth would be blessed (Gen 12:1; 28:15). To lead the Hebrew people out of captivity in Egypt, God selects one main man, Moses, and his brother Aaron. Later he chooses one woman, Esther, to save the children of Israel in captivity under Xerxes.

So it went throughout the history of Israel: individual men and women through whom God worked to bring about the development of his people. But never were the heroes of the Hebrew Scriptures the sole focus. As biblical scholar Walther Eichrodt says, "Old Testament faith knows nothing in any situation or at any time of a religious individualism which gives a man a private relationship with God unconnected with the community either in its roots, its realisation or its goal."[1]

Perhaps the clearest illustration of this combination of individual and corporate is in Psalm 106 (vv. 4-5). The psalmist says,

Remember me, O LORD, when you show favor to your people;
come to my aid when you save them,
that I may enjoy the prosperity of your chosen ones,
that I may share in the joy of your nation,
and join your inheritance in giving praise.

The psalmist does not seek salvation for himself apart from his people. What gives him joy is the joy of "your nation." It is only by being a part of the family of God that he is satisfied.

Community: A New Testament Perspective

The New Testament continues the theme of community. Jesus gathered around him many disciples. From them he selected twelve as apostles. Before his death Peter had emerged as a main figure, and after his resurrection Jesus singled out Peter for leadership (Jn 21:15-19). But the disciples were chastened when they argued about the pecking order in heaven (Mk 9:33-37). Theirs was to be a community of equals who when praying were to say, "*Our* father . . ." (Mt 6:9).

The *church* came into being after the resurrection. It was to be a model of diversity in unity. In unity it was a chosen *race*, a royal *priesthood*, a holy *nation*, God's own *people* (1 Pet 2:9). Jesus prays for this unity in powerful terms:

> My prayer is not for them [the original apostles] alone. I pray also for those who will believe in me through their message, that all of them may be one, Father, just as you are in me and I am in you. May they also be in us so that the world may believe that you have sent me. I have given them the glory that you gave me, that they may be one as we are one: I in them and you in me. May they be brought to complete unity to let the world know that you sent me and have loved them even as you have loved me. (Jn 17:20-23)

In diversity it was to incorporate a very wide group of people with a wide diversity of spiritual gifts, all of which were to be used for the mutual benefit of all (1 Cor 12). In fact, the church was to be like a physical body, with each part having its unique function and value but also working together for the health of the whole organism.

Biblical Realism

We have to be careful here. It is easy to find passages in the Old and New Testaments that either call for or depict what looks like an ideal community. The human heart longs for a home, a place of rest from outside pressures, a place to be what one is without pretense, a place to exercise one's talents and be appreciated for what one is and does.

> How good and pleasant it is
> when brothers live together in unity!
> It is like precious oil poured on the head,

> running down on the beard,
> running down on Aaron's beard,
>> down the collar of his robes.
> It is as if the dew of Mount Hermon
>> were falling on Mount Zion.
> For there the LORD bestows his blessing,
>> even life forevermore. (Ps 133)

But there is no romanticism in Scripture. We are given no encouragement to expect that an ideal community will ever occur this side of glory. Only in heaven will all tears be wiped from our eyes (Rev 21:4).

On earth what we see over and over again is just the opposite. In the Old Testament the people of God were constantly straying from God's intentions for them. Even in Psalm 133, the psalmist seems to express amazement at the glorious oddity of unity under God. At times utter chaos reigned as "everyone did what was right in his own eyes" (Judg 21:25 NKJV).

In the New Testament the disciples quarreled over who would be the greatest in heaven, and in the churches that formed after Jesus' resurrection the apostles found that bitterness and rivalry were constant problems. The opening chapters of Paul's first letter to the Corinthians, for example, pictures a church in dire straits because of a lack of mature community.

One event in the early church in Jerusalem has particular relevance for Christian groups today. The first church in Jerusalem was composed mostly of Jews, but these Jews were divided in their cultural background. Some were Hellenistic (that is, though they were Hebrew by heritage, they primarily spoke the Greek language and reflected the Greek culture), and some were Hebrew (raised in the more traditional form of Jewish culture). The Hellenistic Jews thought that their widows were not being treated equally in food distribution with the Hebrew Jews. The church solved this problem by selecting a group to oversee the distribution of food: seven people "full of the Spirit" representing varied cultural backgrounds (Acts 6:1-7). Here is biblical multicultural community in action.

Not all such problems were solved so easily, as a full reading of Acts and the letters of the apostles shows.

An Alien Community in a Hostile Culture

God's people have in some sense always been an alien community in a hostile culture. Whether we look at the Hebrew people in Egypt or in a Canaan they did not clear of Canaanites, or the early church in a place like Corinth or Rome, we see the people of God surrounded by, even penetrated by, the ethos of what the New Testament calls "the world." And this is the way it should be. Martin Luther put it bluntly: "The Kingdom is to be in the midst of your enemies. And he who will not suffer this does not want to be of the Kingdom of Christ; he wants to be among friends, to sit among roses and lilies, not with the bad people but the devout people. O you blasphemers and betrayers of Christ! If Christ had done what you are doing who would ever have been spared?"[2]

The "community of the king," as Howard Snyder terms the church, is to remain in the closest of contact with the "world" at large. Its task is to be salt and light (Mt 5:13-16), to act as a preservative of the vestiges of good in culture and shine as a beacon to guide men and women into the haven of God's rest.

As such it is a community of the redeemed. There is no sense in which a Christian community can be or should consider itself to be a perfect society. All utopianism, all notion of creating a society in which men and women live in perfect realization of God's will, is to be shunned like the pestilence it truly is.

God hates visionary dreaming; it makes the dreamer proud and pretentious. The man who fashions a visionary ideal of community demands that it be realized by God, by others, and by himself. He enters the community of Christians with his demands, sets up his own law, and judges the brethren and God Himself accordingly. He stands adamant, a living reproach to all others in the circle of brethren. He acts as if he is the creator of the Christian community, as if his dream binds men together. When things do not go his way, he calls the effort a failure. When his ideal picture is destroyed, he sees the community going to smash. So he becomes, first an accuser of his brethren, then an accuser of God, and finally the despairing accuser himself.[3]

As Christians we are united in our fallenness just as in our creation and redemption. God is not done with us yet. Thank God! And let us never forget it. As Bonhoeffer says, Christian community "is not an ideal, but a divine reality, . . . a spiritual and not a psychic reality."[4] God sees us as redeemed, for he has redeemed us. But we are still on the mend. Our fallen natures still obtrude. So the community is a community of hope—of prayers of confession and thanksgiving, of struggle to understand God's will and to obey, of worship of a God whom we see only dimly and strain to see more clearly.

So the stance the community takes within the larger hostile world must never be one of arrogance: "We've made it. Aren't we great? Bet you can't be as good as we are. And, by the way, stay away because we don't want to be contaminated."

Rather, the community takes the humble role of being honest within the community and outside as well. It calls us men and women of all stripes in the world—the lame and halt, the high and mighty, the students flunking out and the star professors winning Nobel prizes—to join them in honoring God. It calls us to take up the cross of Christ, to lose our lives for the sake of Jesus Christ and the good news of the kingdom. It calls each of us to repent and join the community of the redeemed, the community of suffering, to be transformed by the renewing of our minds and then to become agents of transformation, working to bring the values of the kingdom to bear more and more in the workaday life of all people everywhere.

Bonhoeffer again is worth quoting at length:

There is probably no Christian to whom God has not given the uplifting *experience* of genuine Christian community at least once in his life. But in this world such experiences can be no more than a gracious extra beyond the daily bread of Christian community life. We have no claim upon such experiences, and we do not live with other Christians for the sake of acquiring them. It is not the experience of Christian brotherhood, but solid and certain faith in brotherhood that holds us together. That God has acted and wants to act upon us all, this we see in faith as God's greatest gift, this makes us glad and happy, but it also makes us ready to forgo all such experiences when God at times does not grant them. We are bound together by faith not by experience.[5]

Christian Community on Campus

Such a view of community is what Maria Marquez wanted HCF to understand and to strive toward embodying.

She wanted the Christians in HCF to realize that they were not just individuals. There's more to being a campus Christian than hanging around other Christians for some human companionship masquerading as Christian fellowship. Nor is being a disciple of Christ limited to getting to know and then doing God's will for "my life." God's will for each person's life includes God's will for community.

This would include bearing one another's burdens, Maria thought: suffering with the suffering, rejoicing with the rejoicing. It would mean deliberate, intentional, full-orbed fellowship—worshiping together, serving the outer community together, spreading the good news of Jesus Christ together, being a city set on a hill, one everyone could see by its conspicuousness and being one to which people would be drawn by the power of the presence of Christ in its midst. It would mean that those whom God had chosen to be leaders and serve on committees would do so with joy as well as a sense of duty.

Was this utopian? Maria hoped not. She believed it was what Christ would have their student group be.

11
BOB WONG'S
SEARCH FOR JESUS

We believe . . .
Jesus was a good man just like Buddha
Mohammed and ourselves.
He was a good moral teacher although we think
his good morals were bad.
(STEVE TURNER, "CREED")

*C*hris, bonkers over Susie, still kept pretty much on an even keel with his friends. Bill reined him in when he waxed too eloquent over Ms. Wonderful. And Bob kept his mind alert with his continued probing about the Christian faith.

What to do about Bob? How could Chris and Bill make a case for the Christian faith? Bob's faith in atheism was clearly undermined. But how did one bring him from his doubts about atheism to faith in Jesus Christ as Lord and Savior? Chris and Bill decided to ask the speaker at the Hansom Christian Fellowship meeting. She lived near campus; so they set up a long lunch hour with her in the dorm cafeteria.

They began by telling Maria that they wanted to take her teaching about community to heart. Chris especially could already see that because of his friendship with Bill and Bob, life this semester was going much better than before. Now they wanted to know what they could do to help Bob Wong become a Christian.

Maria's advice was simply "Introduce him to Jesus. Just get him to know who he claimed and showed himself to be."

"How do we do that? Preach at him? He'll never go for it. He'll raise questions before we get to point one," Chris retorted.

"No, don't preach at him, with him, on him or about him. Don't preach at all. Ask if he'd be willing to study a Gospel with one or both of you, or maybe with a group of others some of whom, like him, have lots of doubts."

This was a new idea to both Chris and Bill. They thought only Christians would be willing to study the Bible and be able to understand it. When they told Maria that the two of them were already studying the Bible, she encouraged them to invite Bob to join in. Maybe they could even go back to the beginning of Mark and start over. "Or use this study guide." Here Maria dug into her backpack for a guide containing questions on passages selected mostly from the Gospels of Mark and Luke. Its goal was to introduce Jesus to someone who knew little or nothing about Jesus or the basis of the Christian faith.

Chris took the guide, and he and Bill agreed to see if Bob would be willing to study with them. To the surprise of both of them, Bob said yes.

So Chris and Bill put up a notice in the entryway to Chris's dormitory, and they asked a few students, including some they hardly knew, to join them for a study called "Who Was Jesus?" They chose a time when Ralph Imokay said he'd be in the library studying. By 10:00 p.m., the time announced, five people including Chris, Bill and Bob had arrived; ten minutes later three more came. Chris and Bill were stunned.

There they were. John of the Jane-and-John meditating dyad said Jane had to go home for the week and he was lonely. Betty Holden, whom they soon discovered was a member of Hansom State Fellowship and lived in a nearby dorm, wanted to encourage Chris and Bill;

she had led her first dorm Bible study two years ago. Debbie Dobie, who, like Bill, was new to the campus, thought the idea of a Bible study was just weird enough to be fun. Sandy Sollas, her roommate, tagged along. And Sylvester Lentz came because he was genuinely intrigued with the question.

Over the next few weeks other students, including Jane, dropped in and dropped out, but those who had come the first night never missed.

What happens when a person—or a group of people—begins to read the Gospels for what they really say? What happens when students open their eyes to the text and their minds to what they see?

One thing that happens is that their views of Jesus—if they have any—are radically altered. Jesus is just not the person most people think he is. Take the first section from the Gospel of Mark that the students in Chris's room studied—Mark 1:1-34.

Chris started the study by asking the group, "If you were to tell the story of Jesus, where would you begin?"

"With his birth," Debbie said. "I like that story, the manger and all. Mom used to tell it at Christmas."

"With his parents," Bob said. "I bet he made them rather unhappy." Chris knew Bob was reflecting on his own parents and how disappointed they were with him.

"Well, let's see how Mark's Gospel begins the story." Bill directed the group to the Gospel and asked John to read it.

"I guess we were both wrong," Debbie said. "The beginning of the story here is a quotation from a prophet. Who's Isaiah? What's all this about a messenger?"

The conversation was off and running as Chris let various people who thought they knew what was going on make their comments. Often he had to pull the discussion back to the text itself. Bill would sometimes help by asking, "Where does it say that?" Chris began to learn that this was a good way to get the conversation refocused on the issue at hand.

What no one in the room had to do was pretend that they had all the answers. No one needed to be an "expert"; on most important issues the text spoke for itself. When questions no one could answer did arise, Chris jotted them down and tried to have a comment on them by the next meeting.

But no one could avoid the obvious: Jesus was someone very special. The first study pointed out his place in the history of the Jewish people, his special relationship as the "Son" of God, his authority to call disciples (who actually came when he called) to cast out demons and to heal the sick. The story in the Gospel of Mark proceeded so rapidly and yet was so rich in significance that it left the students amazed.

"This was great," Debbie said. "I came 'cause I thought it would be a gas to see just how weird this whole Jesus bit was. And yes it is weird, but not like weird-stupid, like I imagined, but weird-fascinating. I mean, wow! Jesus was really something!"

John, whom Chris had expected to bring up the problem of the sound of one hand clapping, had entered into the discussion quite rationally, Chris thought. Better, he thanked Chris for relieving his loneliness, and Sy who had said nothing all evening left with a curious smile.

But it was Bob whom Bill and Chris were interested in pursuing. What did he think? They were not long in finding out.

"Well, Jesus as Mark tells the story is much different than I thought he was, that's for sure. But I don't see how you can really believe that this story about him is true."

"Just bear with the story a while," Bill said. "Why don't you read on into the Gospel of Mark and see where the story goes?" And Bob did just that. In fact, he went on to read the Gospel of Luke as well, and after that Matthew and John. He didn't know it then, but he was hooked on Jesus.

As the studies proceeded through the weeks following, the course of an argument began to unfold. The questions that Chris asked, many of which were prompted by the guide he was using, kept coming back to one major issue: Who did Jesus think he was? And the answers became more and more extreme as the studies followed the life of Jesus.

Jesus thought he was the one predicted by the prophet Isaiah: the one upon whom rested the Spirit of the Lord, whose task was to "preach good news to the poor, . . . proclaim freedom for the prisoners and recovery of sight for the blind" (Lk 4:17-19). He compared himself with Elijah and Elisha; he was so sure of his own message that he threatened to go to the hated Syrians and Lebanese if his own neighbors would not believe in him. He not only healed a paralytic brought to him on a cot let down through a ceiling so that the man folded up the cot and walked away, but he forgave the man's sins, thus claiming the prerogative of God himself. He accepted the outcast, the prostitutes, the lunatic and diseased, healed them and sent them forth on a new life. He totally reinterpreted the celebration of the Passover feast, and even claimed to be the one whose death would be a sacrifice for the sins of the world. There was the poignant death of a martyr for a cause, a cause all wrapped up in who he claimed to be, the one who gave his life a "ransom for many" (Mk 10:45).

Then there was what to Bob had been simply incredible—the resurrection. That is, it had been incredible to him before he had read the Gospels in their entirety. By the middle of the semester, the resurrection began to look more like the inevitable outcome of the life of a person like this.

At the end of every study Chris would ask, "Okay. Given what we've seen of Jesus tonight, who could he be?" Each week Bob got more and more puzzled. If the claims Jesus was making for himself were not true, he must have been a fraud. Yet Jesus did not act like a fraud. He took no money for his work. He told extremely clever stories. His ethics were more profound than anything Bob had run into in philosophy.

He seemed to make the claims of a crazy man—ability to forgive sins, special knowledge of God, so close a relationship to God he could call him "Abba," or "Daddy." But he was too stable, too healthy in general demeanor, too just plain normal to be crazy. "If this guy is nuts, then we all belong in the loony bin," Bob once replied when John, the only one in the group that Bob thought might himself be insane, had suggested this.

Yet in Jesus' ethics something odd was going on. In the Sermon on the Mount, which Bob read in both texts (Matthew 5—7 and Luke 6), Jesus made extraordinary demands. "You mean," Bob blurted out in one study, "if I'd like to have sex with Sandy here, that makes me an adulterer?"

Sandy bristled, but said nothing. Debbie told him to cool it.

Chris, wondering if the rest of the study was going to be a wash, responded, "No, I don't mean that, but Jesus does."

John, who had been living with Jane for months now, snorted. It was too much for him. *Silly!* But for Bob it was different. Bob had been caught by the lure of Jesus. He had begun to see that when Jesus said something outrageous, it somehow made sense if you thought about it long enough and could begin to see through Jesus' eyes.

He apologized to Sandy and then, as if to make amends to her, flew to Jesus' defense. Before he knew it, Bob was trying to explain to John that in the kingdom of God, righteousness meant purity of thought, singleness of eye, having in mind the very best for others, not for oneself. Just as he got into the swing of his defense of Jesus and was waxing eloquent, he suddenly stopped. The whole group, which had been bursting with energetic comment up to now, became strangely silent. It was dawning on them, including Bob himself, that in his passion Bob had suddenly shifted from the quiet, inquiring, puzzling, ruminating, doubting searcher to a defender of the faith. He couldn't go on. He wasn't there yet.

After that Bob's attitude to his quest for meaning took on a new cast. No, he had not become a believer. He had not yielded his heart and life to Jesus. But his mind was there already. He knew that if he continued gaining information about Jesus, it would simply reinforce what he already grasped just under the threshold of his consciousness. Jesus was the Son of God, the Savior of the world, the Lord of the universe. If he accepted the fact that this was who Jesus was, he would have to change the entire orientation of his life. It would not just be lustful thoughts he'd be forced to try to curb. He would have to repent of a lot more than that. Here thoughts of his parents came to mind.

It made him not sad really, but subdued, and sometimes angry— angry with himself for searching for such a hard truth and finding it, angry with his friends for being his friends. For several weeks he was in a mild depression.

Bob could see that the semester was drawing to a close; two more weeks and he would be free of middle America with its bland blend of religiosity and secularity. He would be back on the West Coast, where he would have a job in a small law firm. His parents had found this job for him. It would be simple clerical work, but they thought it might give him a taste for a good profession.

This sounded good until he remembered two things. First, his parents would be happy to see him lose his atheism, but would be unhappy with either his doubt or the possibility that he was going to turn Christian on them. And worse: Michael Stone, whose atheism had been hardened, if such a thing were possible, at Bertrand College, would be there to challenge him.

Late one evening, Bob was in his room. Kevin had his head buried in his biology text, cramming for the crucial test of the semester. The whole hall was utterly quiet. Bob was down in the deepest depression of his life. Thinking to shake it off, he turned to look again at Jesus. "The hair of the dog that bit me," he muttered to himself.

He'd been reading the Gospel of Matthew lately, and so he flipped it open. Under a section headed "Rest for the Weary" he read, "Come to me, all you who are weary and burdened, and I will give you rest. Take my yoke upon you and learn from me, for I am gentle and humble in heart, and you will find rest for you souls. For my yoke is easy and my burden is light" (Mt 11:28-29).

It was too much. Without repentance, without a softening of his heart, without yielding to the gentle call of Jesus, Bob Wong wept silently. Then suddenly, he looked again at the Bible, took out his pocketknife and, with all the force he could muster, jammed it down into the Gospel. In this Bible from that time on "you will find rest" would be severed from "for your soul."

Kevin, startled, looked up to see Bob stomping out of the room and slamming the door. Kevin looked at the Bible, saw the severed text and breathed a prayer. Then he phoned Chris and Bill.[1]

12
IN THE SPRING A YOUNG MAN'S FANCY

We believe that falling in love
is okay so long as you don't fall too hard.
We believe that if you fall too hard,
you can always get up and slip out the back.
(J. W. SIRE, "CREED II")

W hen Chris wrote his mother that he had met the absolutest, coolest, sweetest, cutest, smartest, kindest, rightest "girl," that he was in fact madly in love with her, he expected his mother to commend him for his great find. She didn't.

"Boy," she wrote, after a fairly warm greeting, "get your feet back on the ground!"

The rest of the letter flowed from that. Chris got the message, and after that he rarely mentioned Susie in his rare letters home. In phone conversations she never came up unless his mother asked. Chris had quickly concluded that mothers, at least his, were not capable of recognizing quality in "girlfriends."

Susie Sylvan was in fact almost everything Chris said she was. She was not a philosopher; in fact, she had little interest in purely abstract thinking. Not that she couldn't do it. She just was not interested.

But Susie was brilliant. She loved people and she understood them. Her vocational goal, as much as she had thought it through, was to be a counselor or teacher. She read every book she could find that told the stories of children with special problems—mental, physical, emotional, parental. She was an excellent student, just as she had been in high school.

In addition to not being impressed with Chris's constant philosophic babbling, Susie had another barrier to overcome before she could really trust Chris enough to consider dating him. She had been living with Cynthia Sharp for five months, and, while Cynthia was easy to get along with, she had posed a challenge to Susie's attitude to men. Susie began to see that Cynthia was right about a lot of things: this is a male-dominated society, women have not had the same opportunities as men, men did consider women sex objects—and more.

"Don't trust men. Sure, some of them are okay. And marriage is certainly not out of the question. But go slow," was the advice she offered one evening after Susie had spent a marvelous time with Chris. Susie knew it wasn't bad advice, even if she could not go along with all of Cynthia's ideas. Cynthia was not a Christian, nor likely to be one in the near future, but she was basically a good person and had become a good friend.

Still, once Susie got over the shock of finding out that Chris was really a Christian, she began to understand him as well—understand, like, more than like . . . love, well, maybe. It just seemed much more than infatuation to her. She had been infatuated with a guy in high school. It just didn't seem like that.

One thing Susie did go slow on. She had deliberately not become involved in Chris's Bible study. Yes, it was just across the hall, but both of them thought it would be a good idea for there to be no distractions when something like the fate of Bob Wong's spiritual life was at stake. And Susie was always a distraction to Chris, as he was to her.

But now Chris and Susie had something they could do together. Distraction was no problem.

As soon as Chris heard from Kevin what had happened to Bob, he knocked on Susie's door. She was bleary-eyed. He was in a panic.

"What should we do?" he asked desperately.

"Let's get the Hansom Christian Fellowship mobilized to pray for Bob." Susie by now was wide awake. "In fact, let me do that. You go and look for Bob."

In fifteen minutes the emergency prayer network of HCF was accessed. The guys who set up the network were computer majors—thus the high-tech language. But the prayer was not high-tech. In five dorms and an apartment off campus, it mounted upward in a serious wave of compassion.

Many of the students in HCF knew Chris and Bill, or at least knew about them. They had been a welcome addition to the group. And many knew about Bob, too, though Bob had never been to an HCF event. So the prayers ascended. A battle was raging in Bob's soul. Unbeknown to him, people he had never met were fighting for his life.

Chris, Bill and Kevin each took part of the campus and went looking for Bob. They had nothing to go on. And they had no success.

Bob was angry and depressed. But he was not going to end it all, as some of the HCFers thought he might. He had simply reached the end of his ability to keep his mind from affecting his will or his emotions. Long ago Bob had given up the confident atheism of Bertrand Russell and the belligerent atheism of Madalyn Murray O'Hair. Now he could maintain neither the constantly questioning stance of Socrates nor the calm, stoic resignation of Cicero—two models Bob had often emulated once he became more agnostic. He had to admit that he was now more like Kierkegaard. The phrases, titles of two of the great Dane's books, swirled together in his mind—*fear and trembling . . . sickness unto death.*

That he was simply an ordinary intelligent human being facing a dilemma common to many people as they wrestle with God never occurred to him. But that's what he was: just a young man facing for the first time the ultimate implications of the claims of Jesus. Hundreds have done it before him. Some, situated where Bob was, have slipped quickly over the threshold into faith and never looked back. Some, having almost tasted the joy of commitment to Christ, have drawn back in a sadness that has turned to anger—an anger that finally spurred them to bitterly attack all who call themselves Christian. Some just slip away, divert themselves with movies, studies, music, sex, sport, the eternal Walkman, and never think about Jesus again.

The noise of the slammed door disturbed a few students, who stuck their heads out to see what had happened. When they saw it was only Bob, they went back to their books or slipped into bed. The noise had startled Bob too. He could see that he had done something dramatic, probably too dramatic really. He couldn't go back and face Kevin, not now. So he headed for a corner in the library courtyard, where the base supporting a reproduction of Rodin's statue *The Thinker* formed a niche just wide enough to slip into and narrow enough not to be easily seen in. There he spent the night, falling asleep with his hand on his chin.

Some in the prayer network stayed up all night; others prayed by turns, catching sleep between their watch. By morning, the search party had not found Bob. As classes began, the network broke up, leaving only Message Central to handle any information.

"Bob!" Chris shouted when Bob walked into philosophy class. "We've been looking for you all over. Where have you been?"

Bob looked down and mumbled something Chris couldn't hear. Seeing that he was not going to say much, Chris slipped away and reported to Message Central. "Bob's okay. I don't know what he did or where he was. But he's okay." Then he slipped back into the room as Prof. Knock called on him.

"Mr. Chrisman, explain Plato's concept of love in the *Symposium*. Is it consistent with Plato's metaphysics?" Chris was astounded by the question's irrelevance to what he had just experienced. For the first time in Knock's class, Chris had nothing to say.

That is, Chris had nothing to say to Prof. Knock. He had lots to ask Bob. And he had lots to say to Susie, who had initiated the prayer network and spent the whole night on her knees.

Bob didn't say much to his friends. He didn't tell them where he had spent the night. He thought, if things got worse, he might have to use this place again. Having sloughed off Kierkegaard, he had returned to Cicero. All he would say to Chris was "I just don't get it. This Jesus thing has had me tied in knots. But I'm resolved now. I'll just keep my mind open." Conversation with him after this was cool and detached.

Bob plunged into his studies and, so far as Chris and Bill could tell, laid aside any personal search for truth. The prayer network dissolved, but Chris, Susie, Bill and Kevin kept up their prayers for him in private.

"In the spring a young man's fancy lightly turns to thoughts of love," Tennyson wrote. But Chris's fancy turned rather more heavily. In his bones Chris knew there was no turning back now.

Still, not much could be done with the fancy. All of them had to plunge into their studies. Only a couple of weeks remained before finals.

13
THE PUBLIC
FACE OF CHRISTIAN FAITH

We believe in putting our faith on the back burner
when it gets too hot on the front one.
We believe in an intense, ecstatic devotion to God
so long as we don't have to give up our stock in Philip Morris.
(J. W. SIRE, "CREED II")

*T*he end of Chris's second semester at Hansom State was in sight.
Late one evening when he had finished his studies, he found
himself unusually exhilarated. He had put the finishing touches
on his paper on *Zen and the Art of Motorcycle Maintenance* and was
excited. He wanted to read it to someone. Susie would be ideal, he
thought. But when he looked across the hall, there was no light under
the door. He figured that Susie wouldn't mind being wakened, but he
was not in the mood for an encounter with her roommate, Cynthia
Sharp.

Chris's own roommate had long been sleeping, and besides, Ralph
had remained, as far as Chris could see, totally uninterested in anything Chris did or thought, let alone wrote. So Chris wandered down
to the lounge, deadly quiet at the end of the semester with everyone
either sleeping or cramming to make intellectual amends before the
final tribunal found them guilty of massive ignorance. Chris got a
Coke from the vending machine and settled into an easy chair.

So this is the end of my first year of college. Chris cast his mind back over the past nine months. *Things are sure different from what I thought they'd be,* he mused. *And I'm different.* Chris's faith was becoming more and more a matter of lifestyle to him, and he thought about the changes it had brought.

One thing struck Chris in particular. Christianity was not just a matter of getting saved and then getting on with life as if nothing else had changed. Everything changed. The way one studied was different. The questions one asked in class were often not asked by anyone else. The way one thought about life after college was different too.

Chris did often think about this, because summer was coming and he'd be back working again—where he didn't know. Still, he knew his attitude would be different from last summer. Then he thought about his roommate. Chris had felt awkward those first few months with Ralph. Now, having been as unobtrusive with his faith as he could be, he was resigned to living with a roommate he couldn't interest in Jesus.

Then he thought about Susie. The way he related to Susie was different too. There was no question in his mind about sleeping with her. That was out—not that he hadn't thought about it, not that it would have been difficult (Susie had thought about it too), not that it wasn't a common practice among the students in his dorm, not even that it was unheard of among his Christian friends. But without ever discussing the subject, both were resolved: the act of physical consummation of love—that was for after marriage. Chris actually began to think about that possibility.

But now, looking beyond the upcoming finals, he faced the summer. Even the summer looked different to him, especially after the talk he'd heard at the large group meeting of Hansom Christian Fellowship a few weeks earlier.

What was now beginning to dawn on Chris is that being a Christian is a full-time affair. It affects every part of life. And the number of parts is almost beyond count.

As a high-school student Chris had attended a church that stayed largely on the margins of society. It addressed the personal needs of the members, took good care of the church family and gave generously to foreign missions. A few members even worked in ministries to the poor in the community. But within the church itself, Chris never heard any talk about the social structures that lead to poverty, or mention of public affairs like the building of housing for low-income people. The fact is that Chris's church was typical of a major stream of Protestant churches, even some entire denominations.

Now Chris was seeing that there is something wrong with this seeming lack of concern. It was the talk by a guest lecturer at HCF that had gotten him thinking like this. The lecturer called his talk "The Ships of Tarshish and the Public Face of Christianity." What follows is the substance of that talk.

Privatization

A large percentage of Americans still attend church on Sunday; many more are church members. But most churches and some whole denominations shun any concern with large portions of American society.

For some segments of Protestant Christianity, this is deliberate. The church's business, says Bob Jones Jr. (whose father founded Bob Jones University in North Carolina), is solely with the message of salvation. Christians, whether laity or clergy, are all to be evangelists, but are to spend no time thinking and working toward the orderly running of society at large.

Other segments of Christianity emphasize these matters at a denominational level or from the pulpit, but find few ordinary parishioners acting on their message. Some churches do become heavily engaged with social welfare programs, but their concern is often limited to binding up the wounded and rescuing those cast out by the system. Little thought or effort is expended in promoting systematic social justice—that is, helping improve the system itself.

This picture is not without exception. Undergraduate institutions like Wheaton College and Calvin College have been on the forefront of combating Christianity's historic weakness at this point. Then too there are graduate institutions like the Institute for Christian Studies (Toronto), Regent College (Vancouver) and New College for Advanced Christian Studies in Berkeley that strongly emphasize the cultural role of the church. And one must note as well individual organizations like Evangelicals for Social Action and the Association for Public Justice and Trinity Forum. The Williamsburg Charter, the outgrowth of an attempt to forge a Christian public philosophy on the issue of religious freedom, is also an illustration.[1]

But by and large in the Western world Christianity has become a private matter.[2] As Os Guinness puts it, *privatization* is "the process by which . . . a cleavage develops between the public and private spheres."[3]

Perhaps this can be made clearer by a diagram.

Figure 1. The Separation Between Public and Private

	PUBLIC		PRIVATE	
Objective	FACT Truth, via the scientific method Mechanism		VALUE Belief Opinion Purpose	Subjective
Social	Government Law Business Business ethics Production (technology) Work Economy Science		Religion Ethics Pleasure Personal ethics Consumption Leisure Lifestyle Theology	Individual

In the *public* arena mechanism, system and fact (truth determined by the scientific method) reign supreme. This is the realm of law, of order determined by objective criteria or public agreement. If one is employed, for example, one is required to work at times controlled by the company. The manufacturing process is governed by the tractability or intractability of the raw materials. One can't make a carburetor out of coal, a stereo system out of steroids or a silk purse out of a sow's ear.

In the *private* arena, on the other hand, there is great freedom. "Value" (subject to the belief of each individual person) is the controlling (or better, *noncontrolling*) principle. Values are seen to be mutable, subject to the opinion of each person, whether arrived at through reflection, social conditioning or whim. In the area of leisure, for example, one can jog, dance, swim, play cards, join an oratorio society or become a couch potato. In Western countries one has almost an infinite choice of which foods to consume, which clothes to wear, which car to drive and which vacation to take.

Most significantly for our purposes here, in religion no one is required to believe anything in particular. Religion is not seen to be governed by immutable truths. Whatever one believes is okay. We have already seen the implications of this in chapter five.

But privatization does not affect religion only. It splits the work of people from the values they hold, whatever those values are.

The effect of this polarization is to segregate various sectors of Western society from each other. For example, take Barney Smith, a typical stockbroker living in a Chicago suburb. He gets up, has his private devotional time of Bible reading and prayer, jogs a couple of miles and then takes the nonstop train to his company's office in the Loop, reading *The Wall Street Journal* as the train hurtles along. Throughout the day he trades stock for his clients, looking to do so by buying low and selling high. Barney's concern is not for the products of the corporations whose stock he is trading (cigarettes, toys, weapons, telephone service, pharmaceuticals); his concern is for the potential long-and short-term profitability of these shares. Will they pay a high dividend over the long haul? Can he sell them for his client at a significantly higher price later on? Can he make a good return for his brokerage firm, in whose profits on trading he participates?

His moral concerns are limited to the laws and ethics of buying and selling (he must not use insider information to turn a profit for his company, for example). The fact that any given corporation or conglomerate is mistreating its employees, polluting the environment or mismanaging its resources is outside his concern, except as it affects the future stock price and dividend. Barney is strongly in favor of getting handguns off the street, but at work he finds it just as easy and legal and business-wise to buy and sell stock of a company manufacturing those handguns as of one providing excellent health care to the poor. Privatization allows, if not encourages, Barney to leave aside any personal scruples he may have about the companies whose stock he recommends to his clients.

If Barney Smith were to join Chris Chrisman's home church, he would never hear from the pulpit or in any church educational program anything that would support him in his desire for legislation to register handguns with the local police.

The handgun issue, one may say, is trivial. Yet former Surgeon General C. Everett Koop has said that shooting is the number-one cause of death among teenagers. Koop, by the way, is one Christian who has integrated his Christian faith with his public life, though not without severe criticism from many in the Christian community.[4]

It's not just the morality of a few issues, like brokering stocks of tobacco companies or of handgun manufacturers, that are seen to be irrelevant to Christian concern. Most public issues—tax laws, zoning, international relations, housing for the poor, unemployment, education, subtle racism—are ignored by most Christians. The exceptions prove the rule: abortion, euthanasia, homosexuality and women's issues. These do attract the attention of what social activists there are in the church. But despite the public attention given groups like Operation Rescue, the fact is that only a very small percentage of American Christians are involved or have more than uninformed opinions on the matters at stake.

The Cosmic Lordship of Christ

Privatization has sapped the moral strength from our society. We receive very little encouragement to put together the private and public sectors of our lives. Job and home are split apart. Our identities, molded by our double environments, split as well, so that we tend to be at least two people: Barney the businessman/Barney the husband, father, Christian.

But this situation is profoundly unbiblical. In simple terms, Jesus Christ is Lord of all. Every area of life is under his reign. The apostle Paul has expressed this notion dramatically. Notice the inclusiveness of Christ's reign because of his role as Creator:

[Christ] is the image of the invisible God, the firstborn over all creation. For by him all things were created: things in heaven and on earth, visible and invisible, whether thrones or powers or rulers or authorities; all things were created by him and for him. He is before all things, and in him all things hold together. (Col 1:15-17)

All things were created by and for Christ. To make it clear that the range of "all things" is exhaustive, Paul explicitly includes "things in heaven and on earth" and then lists "things" that are both "visible" and "invisible." He explicitly identifies some of the invisible things: *thrones, powers, rulers, authorities.* These are terms which in the first century identified social, political and spiritual forces. Christ is Lord over all realms—public and private.

Now notice the inclusiveness of Christ's reign because of his role as Savior:

And he is the head of the body, the church; he is the beginning and the firstborn from among the dead, so that in everything he might have the supremacy. For God was pleased to have all his fullness dwell in him, and through him to reconcile to himself all things, whether things on earth or things in heaven, by making peace through his blood, shed on the cross. (Col 1:18-20)

Christ not only rules over the church but he *reconciles to himself all things*. Jesus Christ is bringing the whole of fallen creation back to himself.

The Ships of Tarshish

If we can get at least a dim picture of what that reconciliation might look like, it will help us see how the public and private sectors of our lives will be both integrated and redeemed.[5]

The Hebrew Scriptures tell the story of the creation, the Fall and the beginning of redemption. They even give a glimpse of glory. The texts about creation are short (Gen 1—2), but reflections on God as Creator and on the world as his creation abound. The psalmist exults:

The heavens declare the glory of God;

the skies proclaim the work of his hands.

Day after day they pour forth speech;

night after night they display knowledge. (Ps 19:1-2)

All the ancient prophets of Israel saw God as Creator and caretaker of the earth. But they also saw God's human creation as fallen and rebellious, and they looked at the earth as corrupted by human sin. In the very beginning of the human race, there was rebellion against God. And so the earth was cursed, men and women would be at each other's throats, pain would accompany childbirth and the sweat of hard labor the growing of crops for food. Death would be the end of each person's sojourn on earth.

The Old Testament is brutally realistic about the evils and agonies of human existence. Men offer up their daughters to rowdies to save their own lives, and they chop up bodies and send them to their neighbors to incite vengeance. A woman drives a tent peg through the forehead of an enemy leader. Eight centuries before Christ, Isaiah, one of the most famous of prophets, saw his time as an abomination:

Surely wickedness burns like a fire;

it consumes briars and thorns,

it sets the forest thickets ablaze,
    so that it rolls upward in a column of smoke.
By the wrath of the LORD Almighty
    the land will be scorched
and the people will be fuel for the fire;
    no one will spare his brother.
On the right they will devour,
    but still be hungry;
on the left they will eat,
    but not be satisfied.
Each will feed on the flesh of his own offspring:
    Manasseh will feed on Ephraim, and Ephraim on Manasseh;
    together they will turn against Judah.
Yet for all this, [God's] anger is not turned away,
    his hand is still upraised. (Is 9:18-21)

The judgment of God on the nation of Israel affected every level of society. There were no innocent noncombatants; men, women and children, cattle and sheep, land and sea were all affected.

Come, all you beasts of the field,
    come and devour, all you beasts of the forest!
Israel's watchmen are blind,
    they all lack knowledge;
they are all mute dogs,
    they cannot bark;
they lie around and dream,
    they love to sleep. (Is 56:9-10)

The only peace the righteous get in a society like the one Isaiah describes is the peace of death.

The righteous perish,
    and no one ponders it in his heart;
devout men are taken away,
    and no one understands
that the righteous are taken away

to be spared from evil.
Those who walk uprightly
   enter into peace;
they find rest as they lie in death. (Is 57:1-2)

At the same time that Isaiah is picturing the agonies of his own day, he envisions the ecstasies of God's future city—Zion set on a hill and filled with the glory of God.

Arise, shine, for your light has come,
   and the glory of the LORD rises upon you.
See, darkness covers the earth
   and thick darkness is over the peoples,
but the LORD rises upon you
   and his glory appears over you.
Nations will come to your light,
   and kings to the brightness of your dawn. (Is 60:1-3)

Isaiah then sees the sons and daughters of Israel flooding back to Zion, and with them flocks of sheep from Kedar and herds of camels from Sheba, "bearing gold and incense and proclaiming the praise of the LORD" (vv. 4-7). Then come the ships of Tarshish:

Who are these that fly along like clouds,
   like doves to their nests?
Surely the islands look to me;
   in the lead are the ships of Tarshish,
bringing your sons from afar,
   with their silver and gold,
to the honor of the LORD your God,
   the Holy One of Israel,
   for he has endowed you with splendor.
Foreigners will rebuild your walls,
   and their kings will serve you. (Is 60:8-10)

"What are the ships of Tarshish doing here?" theologian Richard Mouw asks. Why is the wealth of foreign nations being brought into Zion? Before we answer this question, we should look at the vision of the Holy City in Revelation 21. Here the writer John describes what he saw "in the Spirit" (Rev 4:2): "Then I saw a new heaven and a new earth, for the first heaven and the first earth had passed away, and there was no longer any sea. I saw the Holy City, the new Jerusalem, coming down out of heaven" (Rev 21:1-2). An angel is seen measuring the city: fourteen hundred miles long, fourteen hundred miles wide and fourteen hundred miles high—a giant cube. "The wall was made of jasper, and the city of pure gold, as pure as glass" (v. 18). Here is a transcendent city fashioned in the heavens and let down toward earth.

John, the author of Revelation, has picked up the imagery of Isaiah. But instead of seeing Zion as a city on earth, as Isaiah seems to do, John sees the Holy City as transcendent, something from the outside, let down "from above." "The glory of God gives it light, and the Lamb is its lamp. The nations will walk by its light, and the kings of the earth will bring their splendor into it" (Rev 21:23-24).

So, then, what are the foreign ships and foreign kings doing in the Holy City? Mouw believes, and I agree, that these ships that come from afar and the kings who "serve" in the city represent "the gathering-in of human cultural 'filling.' Both Isaiah and John link the entrance of the kings to this transaction. The kings of the earth will bring 'the wealth of nations' into the Holy City."[6]

There is much mystery here, much that is not clear, and I do not want to speculate unnecessarily. Nonetheless, the point is made: the wealth of nations belongs in the Heavenly City. Something of what is done and said in the cultural realm will be brought in as part of the furniture of heaven.

It is easy for many of us to think that Handel's *Messiah* will be sung in the heavenlies. Bach's Brandenburg Concertos will surely make it, others may add. I'd like to think we will have some of the music of Thelonius Monk and Dave Brubeck. But there also will be vestiges of political order and the "little acts of kindness and of love" that Wordsworth speaks of.

Mouw refers us to Matthew 20:25-28, in which Jesus transforms "the patterns of human authority."[7] "You know that the rulers of the Gentiles lord it over them, and their high officials exercise authority over them. Not so with you. Instead, whoever wants to become great among you must be your servant, and whoever wants to be first must be your slave—just as the Son of Man did not come to be served, but to serve, and to give his life as a ransom for many."

Then Mouw comments:

[Jesus] calls us to cast our lot with the lowly ones, to identify with the poor and the oppressed of the earth. To live in this manner is to anticipate the coming political vindication, when 'the least one shall become a clan, and the smallest one a mighty nation' (Isa. 60:22). . . . We can act politically in the full assurance that our political deeds will count toward the day of reckoning that will occur in the transformed City. . . . Since we are already citizens of God's commonwealth, we must find effective ways of living in political conformity to its norms and patterns. . . . [And we can call today's political authorities] to perform that kind of ministry which God requires of all who administer human affairs.[8]

The Public Face of Christianity:
Being What We Should Be Where We Are

In our attempt to understand the full sweep of biblical history from creation and Fall to redemption and glory, we must not overlook redemption. That may appear to be what I have done by shifting from Isaiah to Revelation. But the way from the agony of human existence in a fallen world to the ecstasy of eternal life in the Holy City leads through the cross. And the cross is a reality not just for Jesus the Savior, it is a reality for the church.

Jesus came proclaiming, "The time has come. . . . The kingdom of God is near. Repent and believe the good news!" (Mk 1:15). There is a sense in which with Jesus the kingdom of God is already beginning to be realized. His actions are the actions of a person living totally within the framework of the kingdom of God, the lifestyle of the Holy City lived out in the context of the fallen world. Living this lifestyle, totally motivated by the ethics of the kingdom, put Jesus on the cross.

This was thought to be the end of the affair. People could now go back to their own ways. Instead, this death was the eternal once-for-all sacrifice that would pave the way for all people (should they accept the conditions) to be reconciled to God, to be transformed by the renewing of their minds and the sanctification of their lives and to be welcomed into the Holy City as full citizens of the kingdom of God.

First, however, they must simply follow Jesus, and that means taking up his cross as their own. Jesus put it this way: "If anyone would come after me, he must deny himself and take up his cross and follow me. For whoever wants to save his life will lose it, but whoever loses his life for me and for the gospel will save it" (Mk 8:34-35).

John Howard Yoder has said, "Only at one point, only on one subject—but then consistently, universally—is Jesus our example: in his cross. . . . The believer's cross must be, like his Lord's, the price of his social nonconformity; . . . It is the social reality of representing in an unwilling world the Order to come."[9]

The point is that, while the mission of Jesus was to reconcile the world to himself (2 Cor 5:19), he showed us how a reconciled person should act. We should live as he did, displaying by our lives the righteousness of the kingdom of God—kingdom values. The fullest single expression of these values is the Sermon on the Mount (Mt 5—7), but Jesus' parables elaborate these ideas, showing them in action, and the closing section of each of Paul's letters gives much to guide us as well.

The public face of Christianity has not been seen much. Christians are, of course, everywhere. From the high reaches of public office to the boardrooms of major corporations, from the exalted sphere of star professors to the laboratories of top research institutes, from natural science to social science to the humanities, from the fields of wheat to the shop floors of automotive manufacturers: Christians have permeated every field. But where is the evidence of their presence? As Guinness says, "It's not that [Christians] are not where they should be, but that *they aren't what they should be where they are.*"[10]

This then is the challenge of our age: to be what we should be where we are! To put a public face on Christianity, to be a light set on a hill, to be, as Lesslie Newbigin says, a *sign*, an *instrument* and a *foretaste* of God's sovereignty over all the nations, over every realm of life.[11]

The Awesome Task

Chris Chrisman could only remember the outlines of the biblical picture we have just seen here. But he knew that to be a Christian meant some kind of engagement with the world around him. One couldn't be a serious Christian in college and not see that. That was the problem facing him now.

Chris had come to the lounge with energy to burn. His ruminations had now not only drained all that energy but also raised the specter of discouragement. The world was so bad off. There were so many parts to life, so much to bring under the lordship of Christ. Yes, he was ready to do what he could. But there was just too much to do.

Suddenly, something Maria Marquez had said struck him. She had spoken on community. "You're not alone," she said. "You are in this together. Each of you has a spiritual gift. Some of you have several. Each of you is responsible for the role to which God has called you. None of you is responsible for everything. At the end of the day, when you have done what God has called you to do, you can go to bed and sleep well."

Chris liked that idea. This evening he had done well, he thought. His English paper was done on time. In it he had reached a conclusion that brought together the best of his knowledge of theology, philosophy and literature. He had more questions, but this paper had satisfied him even if it would not satisfy his professor. He was willing to take his lumps as well as the kudos he usually received.

Then just as he was about to leave the lounge, he had what afterward he told his friends was perhaps a vision. He wasn't sure. What dawned on him in almost visual terms was that he, Chris, was just a part of God's plan for history. He saw, envisioned, imagined—Chris wasn't sure which—the whole history of earth spread out before him: creation, Fall, the thousands of years intervening, the call of Abraham, the exodus from Egypt, the birth, life, death, resurrection of Jesus, the formation and growth of the church around the world, the coming of Jesus, the judgment of humanity, the heavenly city let down on earth, the ships of Tarshish sailing to Zion, the kings bringing into the city the wealth of the nations.

At first, Chris himself was standing outside the vision, looking in on it. Then, wondering where he was in all of this, he focused his attention on one part that looked like now. There he was, standing in a room looking at a vision like the one he was just seeing. A vision within a vision. Chris was afraid to look for himself in the new vision. He knew he'd see another just like it.

On the one hand he seemed so small. He saw himself as one tiny person in a vast, countless company of men and women that spread themselves from past through present to future: the human dimension of the kingdom of God, set first in the context of the earth and its history and then in the larger frame of what Chris took to be the cosmos.

On the other hand, he could hardly believe he was there in that company. It made him feel both humble and proud. Here he was, one single person, that's all. No, not all: one single person with links to the entire kingdom of God.

With a heart swelling with worship, Chris crept off to bed. This was enough for one night. It was more than enough. Chris was mostly a left-brain person, largely characterized by rational thought. It was the only such vision Chris would ever have. It was enough for a lifetime.

14
THE THINKER
PRAYS

We believe in believing
so long as that's all we have to do.
(J. W. SIRE, "CREED II")

*T*he last meetings of the Hansom Christian Fellowship and
Chris's Bible study put a fitting close to the year. Chris looked
forward to the first of them, but not the second. He was wor-
ried about Bob. Would he come? Had the pressure on him been too
great? Was he already so settled back behind his stoic mask that the
pretense of distancing himself from personal engagement had become a solid reality? The large group meeting took place first.

The main task it had to accomplish was the election of officers for
next year. There hadn't been enough time in the semester, Maria
Marquez thought. The Hansom Christian Fellowship would have to
nominate and elect next year's leaders in the last meeting of the
semester. She hated to think what her supervisor would think of that
when she reported it.

It wasn't that she hadn't tried to get the chapter to think about
leaders for next term. But it was only after she spoke on community

that she was able to get the current leaders to appoint a nominating committee. Finally a slate of officers had been proposed.

President: Walker F. Abraham

Vice president: Nancy B. Holden

Treasurer: Carol P. Adams

Large group coordinator: Alice K. Bentley

Small group coordinator: Kevin B. Leaver

Prayer coordinator: Susan R. Sylvan

Evangelism coordinator: Graham R. Williams

Book table coordinator: William D. Seipel

The meeting began with lots of singing. A week of exams remained, but this was to be the last time the whole fellowship would be together till the fall. Then elections took place, and the slate of candidates was confirmed by the group.

Maria's friend Becky Baldwin, a piano major as an undergraduate and now a campus staff member at nearby Cabot College, spoke on "Making the Summer Count for Christ." She encouraged the new slate of officers to attend the "chapter camp" scheduled for late June in a beautiful retreat center on a lake in Michigan. She charged the whole group with the responsibility of being disciples of Christ wherever they were this summer. Graham and Alice were going on a mission project to Minsk, in the new Belarus. Some others were taking a four-week discipleship training program in Colorado, run by the national organization of which their group was a part. But most, like Chris and Bill, were going home to work. Becky had different suggestions for students in each group, but everyone was encouraged to read Christian books. She suggested one a week and handed out an annotated list.

Afterward Bill and Chris headed for the book table at the back of the room. This was to be Bill's responsibility next term; everyone knew that he and Chris were the big readers in the group. Bill had in fact read some of the recommended books while he was a student at Cornton. Both chose five books they hadn't yet read.

The excitement of the final meeting of HCF cooled when Chris contemplated the final meeting of his dorm Bible study. Every study that semester had been different, and most of them had left Chris somewhat puzzled. In addition to the regulars who had come to the first study, various others had dropped in and out. At each session there had been someone new.

One was Abraham Knox, the student whose aggressive evangelism at the beginning of the year had so turned off Chris and everyone else in the dorm. "Ob," as in "Ob Noxious," the name that Phil Corper had pinned on Abraham one day in the lounge, flopped down on Chris's bed and throughout the study made snide remarks. He had lost his faith by the end of the first semester, when he came to be the laughingstock of the dorm, but now he was more obnoxious than ever. Chris was anguished over the apparent effect of Ob's intrusions. What he didn't know is that Ob's comments were so outrageous that they actually lent credibility to the Gospels. The other study members were more impressed with Jesus than ever.

Another interloper was Jane, John's other half. She had wondered why John kept attending the study after she had returned to campus. The only thing that attracted her was Jesus' prayer life. She investigated this a bit on her own, but couldn't make much of it. What did Jesus do when he went off alone early in the morning to pray? The one prayer she knew he prayed was the one in the Garden of Gethsemane, and this didn't attract her at all. What was he doing wrestling with God? Why didn't he just meditate and find himself absorbed into the divine One?

Then there was the Lord's Prayer. That, she thought at first, might have some promise. But when she and John actually tried meditating on this prayer, chanting it over and over like a mantra, she got the funny feeling that this was not right to do. There was far too much content to this prayer, far too much recognition of a God beyond, a Father in heaven, one whom the prayer acknowledged as special, holy, separate from her and John. It spoke of God's kingdom and his getting what he wanted. It spoke of "debts" in one version and "trespasses" in another. It just wasn't like "Om mane padme hum," a set of untranslatable Sanskrit words which even if translated were only an image—"the jewel in the center of the lotus," some translations read. She soon gave it up.

John had continued chanting the Lord's Prayer on his own. To him there was something real about it. He was beginning to think that maybe Jesus had a better way of getting through to God than he and Jane did.[1] He had not yet tumbled to the fact that the Lord's Prayer was actually not Jesus' own prayer but the prayer he taught his disciples. That would come later.

Debbie Dobie and Sandra Sollas had both become interested in Jesus, and, Chris was happy to note, had also become friends with Susie. They even attended a couple of HCF meetings before the semester was over. Still, they seemed to Chris and Bill some distance from coming to new life in Christ.

Sy Lentz—well, he was a special puzzle. He just never said a thing. His enigmatic smile seemed glued on. Yet he was always there.

Even Chris's roommate, Ralph Imokay, appeared one week, not needing to spend that evening in the library. He found himself contributing despite his plan just to listen. But always after that he stayed away. When Chris asked him about this, he got a quick answer: "Remember? Leave your Bible on your side of the room. Okay?"

"Yeah, okay," Chris said with as little dejection as he could muster.

Finally there was Bob Wong, the reason for the Bible study in the first place. Bob had kept to himself since the incident with the pocketknife. After philosophy class he would talk seriously to neither Chris or Bill. Everything was academic or disengaged from himself. He had come to one more Bible study after his evening at the feet of *The Thinker,* but he had only made observations, astute ones to be sure, about the text and not said a word about implications.

So there was great anxiety as Chris prepared the final Bible study and prayed with Bill and Susie about it. When 10:00 p.m. came and

Bob wasn't there, Chris decided to begin without him. This would be the saddest study of the year.

The room was all but full. One chair was left vacant for Bob. But the tone of the discussion was subdued. Only Chris and Bill were really missing Bob, only they were concerned. But their worry had translated into a gloom that spread to the corners of the room. It was as if a thick wool blanket had settled a few feet above everyone's heads.

Then Bob burst in and filled the room with light. He was trying to control himself, but he couldn't conceal his excitement. He was smiling, smiling so broad a smile that if it hadn't been sparked by so much joy it would have hurt.

"Wow!" said Debbie. "What happened to you?"

Chris guessed to himself. He was right.

"I've just realized who Jesus is," Bob began. "I mean, I have known for some time, but I've just been willing to accept it for what it really means."

"You mean you—the doubter, the skeptic, the spittin' image of old Berty Russell—have become like these guys here?" John exploded, waving his arms toward Chris and Bill.

"I guess so," Bob said somewhat sheepishly, still with a smile so big he could hardly form the words.

"When did all this happen? Did you get your libido under control?" Sandra asked, remembering Bob's near admission of lust for her earlier on.

"It had nothing to do with that, really. That whole thing—seeing Jesus' demands as almost impossible to live by—that's not the point. At least it's not the first point. The first point is that I saw that Jesus had me pegged. He knew me better than I knew myself. I mean he *knows* me better than I know myself. He's alive, you know!" Bob was beginning to spit it all out.

In the next twenty minutes Bob recounted to his friends what had happened. He told all of them about the evening he'd stabbed the

Bible with his knife. He told them where he'd spent that night. (Chris and Bill hadn't heard about this before.) He recounted his attempt to play it cool, to pretend that he could treat Jesus as he treated Socrates, as a sage worth learning from. Then he told them about the break-through.

On the outside Bob had returned to the stoic model of Cicero; inside, he had been more Kierkegaardian than ever. "Sickness unto death" and "fear and trembling" were no longer exaggerated phrases. There was nothing more Bob needed to know about Jesus or God or the Bible. He only needed to submit to what he knew was the truth.

Bob had seen both the value and the limitations of human reason in making a case for the Christian faith. Through his philosophic dialogues with Chris and Bill he had seen how reason helps to clarify problems and even leads to a recognition of its own limitations. Human reason itself rests on faith in the mind's capacity to discern the difference between truth and falsity when the issues were clear. It even takes faith in one's own judgment to conclude that "A is A" is true and "A is not-A" not true.

Even formal logic requires faith. But even if formal logic is a tool for all useful thought, it doesn't fill the A with content. What *is* A? . . . and B and C and D, ad infinitum? Formal logic does not supply that. Nor does reason more broadly conceived seem to supply any certain propositions from which to argue. Experience seems to supply some, but experience, when it comes to matters of value and general rules for life, varies so much from person to person, culture to culture, that it seems to give little help. Everyone's ideas of God and their religious experiences or lack of them are just too disparate to be of much help.

Bob was illustrating a principle he couldn't yet articulate: reason's most important function in apologetics and evangelism today is to clear away the objections to Christian faith, so that a person becomes willing to look at the positive evidence that comes through clearly from revelation. And what comes through most convincingly is Jesus. Jesus himself is the best reason for believing in Jesus.

The truth is seen only by those who come to the Gospels with open eyes, open ears, open minds and open hearts. Without this the Bible remains a closed book even when it is open before us. But we do not have to have perfect vision to begin to glimpse the majesty and mystery of Jesus. Often just a peek at him will so startle us that our eyes spring open, our ears perk up, our minds turn on and our hearts begin to melt.

Bob recounted how that melting occurred in him. It had happened that very evening. Long before darkness had settled in, now that it was the end of May, he had decided to return to *The Thinker*. Again he wedged himself into the narrow niche at the base of the statue. Again he placed his hand on his chin and traced in his mind the contours of his search for truth. Again he saw where it all led.

When he had done this, there seemed to him nothing left to do but admit it was all so. And that's what he did. He removed his right hand from his chin and placed it with his left in what he had seen was the traditional way Christians pray. Then he poured out to God the anguish of his heart: the sorrow for his sin, the rebellion against his parents, the arrogance of his philosophic mind, the lust for Sandy and lots of other women students as well (this had been a private matter, only hinted at in his outburst in the Bible study), his desire to run his own life. He yielded his mind and heart to Jesus the Truth and the Life. Then he prayed the Lord's Prayer as best as he could remember it. It had fascinated him as much as it had John.

"Come to me," Jesus said, "and I will give you rest." Bob believed that would happen. And it did. And more too. Joy. His eyes were moist when he left *The Thinker*. His heart was overflowing as he almost ran to the Bible study.

Bob's story put all notion of a Bible study out of everyone's mind. Chris and Bill were ecstatic. John was astounded. *There really is something behind this Lord's Prayer after all,* he concluded. Debbie and Sandy were pleased but puzzled. *Is this what becoming a Christian is like?* Sandy thought to herself. As Chris said to Bill later, "Did you notice? Even Sy wiped the silly grin off his face."

That night turned into morning before, one by one, the group members slipped off to bed, where inner dialogues kept most of them awake for hours. Bob and Bill stayed for a long time with Chris. Rejoicing turned to prayers of thanks and prayers for Bob as he faced the summer.

The three would now be split up. Bill would work in McDonald's, where he had spent his summers in high school. Bob would return to Mendocino.

There, he knew, he would face his parents. And what to do? What to say? He knew he had to somehow begin to see them as *his parents,* to "honor" them, to show this in a way they with their Chinese and Buddhist heritage would recognize. How was he to do this? He didn't know. He was hoping that the law office he would work in would provide relief. He didn't yet know that one of the law partners would be a believer.

And what was he to say to Michael Stone? He couldn't just pick up the conversation where it had left off nine months earlier. He had radically changed. What had happened to Michael? After the first couple of months they had not written to each other. But he expected that in Michael he would face a rock of resistance to anything religious.

And Chris? Well, Chris would look for a job of some kind. He didn't know what it would be yet. He would spend some of his evenings— well, every evening he could—with Susie. Her family lived only thirty minutes' drive from his.

Finals week drew to a close. Soon Susie would be off to the HCF chapter camp for a week of planning for next year. At least she hadn't gone on a foreign mission—not this summer, maybe next. Susie's parents had already come to campus, loaded their station wagon with her things, stuffed Susie herself into a corner of the rear seat and left for home.

Chris, who had his last exam on the last day of finals week, turned to give the campus one last look as his mother eased her car into the traffic headed for Central City.

His mother broke his reverie: "So, tell me about this Susie you're so smitten by."

Though Chris had quit mentioning his love life in his letters and calls home, his mom had remembered all along about his thing for Susie. This was going to be a long summer.

Afterword

"And let the gentle-hearted reader be under no apprehension whatsoever," Anthony Trollope says part way into *Barchester Towers*. "It is not destined that Eleanor shall marry Mr. Slope or Bertie Stanhope."

Many times in this book I have wanted to say the same kind of thing. "Dear Reader, don't worry. Chris Chrisman is not going to lose his faith for good. Bob Wong is not going to remain forever on the outside looking in. Cynthia Sharp is not just a sword to cut away Chris's view of women."

"There are eight million stories in the naked city," one TV voice-over used to say each week. "This has been one of them."

Chris Chrisman is one story, a story I chose to tell largely from the point of view of Chris Chrisman and Bob Wong. Even with the running commentary, I haven't been able to say all I have wanted to say.

Missing is the perspective of Kevin Leaver, the Christian student whose bent toward medicine is not so single-minded as it looks. Missing is Cynthia Sharp's keen insight into the way traditional social structures and language not only unwittingly shape character but also empower some parts of society and oppress others. Missing as well is a critique of overblown Political Correctness. Neither do we see Susie Sylvan's struggle to be a fully Christian woman in the immediate context of Cynthia's anti-Christian version of feminism.

There are no tales of Hansom Christian Fellowship's corporate struggle with community or with the world outside its own bounds. Though Maria Marquez has spoken about community and broached the subject of privatization and the cosmic lordship of Christ, we do not see these issues worked out in action.

Dear Reader, there are many stories in Hansom State University that remain untold. The summer produced many changes in the characters we have met. The fall produced even more. The Knights of Jesus, minus Abe Knox, who remained out of fellowship with them, sponsored an antigay rally. Graham Williams, the evangelism coordinator of Hansom Christian Fellowship, revealed to the group that he had been a practicing homosexual. Cynthia Sharp, though not herself a lesbian, became a spokesperson for the gay-lesbian cause and attacked the Knights of Jesus for its antigay bias and HCF for its removal of Graham from a leadership position.

Just imagine the stories that could be unfolded by the right storyteller.

Notes

Chapter 1: Chris Chrisman Goes to State
[1]Harlan Hatcher says in introducing Anthony Trollope's *The Warden* and *Barchester Towers*, "The spirit of Trollope's fiction is generally one of gentle comedy. There is no sharp or vitriolic satire as in Thackeray, no deep-dyed villain as in Dickens. For Trollope is a friendly man. Like his contemporaries, he invented tag names to identify the dominant characteristics of many of his people, but they sound the comic rather than the satiric note: Mrs. Lookaloft, Mrs. Quiverful, Dr. Anticant, Mr. Sentiment, even Mrs. Proudie" ([New York: Modern Library, 1950], p. xi.) There is much in the university today that merits the vitriol of Thackeray and the unmasking of villainy of Dickens. No lie, Dean Bent was the real name of the dean of one of the graduate schools I attended (and graduated from). Only Thackeray and Dickens could do him justice.

But consider the story in this book rather in the vein of Trollope. With regard to matters other than tone, make no further comparisons.

Chapter 2: The Vortex of Modernity
[1]Carl Sagan, *Cosmos* (New York: Random House, 1980), p. 4.

[2]James Rachels, *The Elements of Moral Philosophy* (New York: Random House, 1986), p. 140.

[3]Richard Rorty, *Contingency, Irony and Solidarity* (Cambridge, U.K.: Cambridge University Press, 1989), p. 67.

[4]Ibid., pp. 151-52.

[5]Oden tells parts of his story in the third person in *After Modernity . . . What?* (Grand Rapids, Mich.: Zondervan, 1990), pp. 26-29, from which the quotations in this and following paragraph have been drawn.

Chapter 4: Chris Chrisman Becomes a Student

[1]At this point in his academic life, Chris has become a true student. Very few college "students" ever do. True students are interested in learning not just to pass a course, or get a degree, or train for a job. Rather, they see their academic work as giving them insight into the way the world really is, or at least the way those who have thought about it and studied it think it is. They are interested in integrating the way they think about one thing with the way they think about another and connecting the way they live with the way they think. True students make no distinction between formal academic study and personal study. They remain students throughout their lives.

Chapter 5: Truth: A Mobile Army of Metaphors

[1]Indeed, a much *more* sophisticated analysis is merited. Fortunately, an excellent, sophisticated but eminently readable book on relativism was published in the early nineties, the best to date: Harold A. Netland, *Dissonant Voices* (Grand Rapids, Mich.: Eerdmans, 1991). There would be many more references to Netland's work in what follows if I had not been so far along in my own analysis before I read his book. See also Lesslie Newbigin's superb treatment of the same topic from a different, more sociological and theological angle: *The Gospel in a Pluralist Society* (Grand Rapids, Mich.: Eerdmans, 1989); Gavin D'Costa, ed., *Christian Uniqueness Reconsidered* (Maryknoll, N.Y.: Orbis Books, 1990), especially essays by Wolfhart Pannenburg (pp. 96-106) and Lesslie Newbigin (pp. 135-48); and S. Mark Heim, "Pluralism and the Otherness of World Religions," *First Things*, August-September 1992, pp. 29-35.

[2]John Henry Cardinal Newman, "The Idea of a University," in *English Prose of the Victorian Era*, ed. Charles Frederick Harrold and William D. Templeman (New York: Oxford University Press, 1938), pp. 575 and 593-94.

[3]See Alasdair MacIntyre's clear analysis in *After Virtue* (Notre Dame, Ind.: University of Notre Dame Press, 1984), pp. 56-61.

[4]See, for example, George Barna, *What Americans Believe* (Ventura, Calif.: Regal Books, 1991), pp. 200-203.

[5]Friedrich Nietzsche, "On Truth and Lie in an Extra-Moral Sense," in *The Portable Nietzsche*, ed. Walter Kaufmann (New York: Viking, 1954), p. 46. Also quoted by Richard Rorty in *Contingency, Irony and Solidarity* (Cambridge, U.K.: Cambridge University Press, 1989), p. 17.

[6]Richard Rorty has abandoned any notion that one can know the truth of anything. "Truth is a property of linguistic entities, of sentences"; it conveys no knowledge of

objective reality. Truth is rather whatever we can get away with saying: "A liberal society is one which is content to call 'true' (or 'right' or 'just') whatever the outcome of undistorted communication happens to be, whatever view wins out in a free and open encounter" (ibid., p. 67).

[7]Barna, for example, says that over 50 percent of Americans believe that "Christians, Jews, Muslims, Buddhists and others all pray to the same God, even though they use different names for God" *(What Americans Believe,* pp. 210-12).

[8]Joseph Campbell with Bill Moyers, *The Power of Myth* (New York: Doubleday, 1988), p. 54-55; Robert Segal, *Joseph Campbell: An Introduction,* rev. ed. (New York: Mentor, 1990), pp. 66-70.

[9]Joseph Campbell with Michael Toms, *An Open Life* (New York: Harper & Row, 1989), p. 50; Segal, *Joseph Campbell,* pp. 27, 30-53, 245-63.

[10]Campbell and Moyers, *The Power of Myth,* p. 25; see also pp. 21, 31, 47, 56, 99, 188 and 190. Segal, *Joseph Campbell,* pp. 85, 116-18. Segal, in addition, notes that Campbell held "an embittered hostility toward his boyhood Roman Catholicism, which he damns for stymying his true, individualistic rather than institutionalized nature of spirituality; an even more unsettling hostility toward Judaism, which in almost antisemitic fashion he caricatures as chauvinistic and literalistic; and . . . a later disdain for the East, which he similarly caricatures as totalitarian and barbaric" (ibid., pp. 23-24).

[11]Ibid., p. 166; see also p. 199.

[12]Stanley J. Samartha is a contemporary exponent of the attempt to circumvent the exclusive claims for each religion. See his essay "The Cross and the Rainbow" in *The Myth of Christian Uniqueness,* ed. John Hick and Paul F. Knitter (Maryknoll, N.Y.: Orbis Books, 1987), pp. 69-88.

[13]Sri Ramakrishna, *The Sayings of Sri Ramakrishna,* ed. Swami Abhedananda (New York: Vedanta Society, 1903), as quoted by Huston Smith, *The Religions of Man* (New York: Harper & Row, 1986), pp. 115-16. John Hick in the Gifford Lectures gives a similar picture in Western, Kantian terms (noumena and phenomena):

> Each of these two basic categories, God and the Absolute, is schematised or made concrete within actual religious experience as a range of particular gods or absolutes. These are, respectively, the *personae* and the *impersonae* in terms of which the Real is humanly known. And the particularising factor . . . is the range of human cultures, actualising different though overlapping aspects of our immensely complex human potentiality for awareness of the transcendent. It is in relation to different ways of being human, developed within the civilizations and cultures of the earth, that the Real, apprehended through the concept of God, is experienced specifically as the God of Israel, or as the Holy Trinity, or as Shiva, or as Allah, or as Vishnu. . . . And it is in relation to yet other forms of life that the Real, apprehended through the concept of the Absolute, is experienced as Brahma, or as Nirvana, or as Being, or as Sunyata. . . . On this view our various religious languages—Buddhist, Christian, Muslim, Hindu . . . each refer to a divine phenomenon or configuration of divine phenomena. When we speak of a personal God, with moral attributes and purposes, or when we speak of the non-personal Absolute, Brahman, or the Dharmakaya, we are speaking of the Real as humanly

experienced: that is, as phenomenon. *(An Interpretation of Religion* [London: Macmillan, 1989], pp. 245-46)

Harold Netland, who studied under John Hick at Claremont School of Religion, has made a profound analysis and critique of Hick's peculiar form of relativism (see Netland, *Dissonant Voices*, esp. pp. 198-233).

[14]See Newbigin's critique in *The Gospel in a Pluralist Society*, p. 161.

[15]Wilfred Cantwell Smith, "Idolatry in Comparative Perspective," in *The Myth of Christian Uniqueness*, ed. John Hick and Paul F. Knitter (Maryknoll, N.Y.: Orbis Books, 1987), p. 55.

[16]Tom Driver, "The Case for Pluralism," in *The Myth of Christian Uniqueness*, p. 212.

[17]Newbigin, *The Gospel in a Pluralist Society*, p. 162.

Chapter 6: Closing a Mind So Open That Everything Falls Out

[1]Alfred, Lord Tennyson, "Prologue," in *In Memoriam A. H. H.*

[2]I have discussed this at some length in a chapter on nihilism in *The Universe Next Door* (Downers Grove, Ill.: InterVarsity Press, 1988), pp. 85-106.

[3]Lesslie Newbigin, *The Gospel in a Pluralist Society* (Grand Rapids, Mich.: Eerdmans, 1989), p. 50.

[4]See Richard Rorty, "Introduction: Pragmatism and Philosophy," in *The Consequences of Pragmatism* (Minneapolis: University of Minnesota Press, 1982), pp. xii-xlvii, for a presentation of this view by a proponent.

[5]Charles Taylor, "Rorty in the Epistemological Tradition," in *Reading Rorty* (Oxford, U.K.: Blackwell, 1990), p. 258.

[6]Many, if not most, of those philosophers who hold such views are nontheists or atheists, at least in the sense that they do not believe that there is a God "out there" who has created the universe and us, or who is actively communicating to us or engaged in undergirding our communication with each other.

[7]Richard Rorty, *Contingency, Irony and Solidarity* (Cambridge, U.K.: Cambridge University Press, 1989), pp. 6-7.

[8]Nietzsche, p. 46; also quoted in Rorty, *Contingency, Irony and Solidarity*, p. 17.

[9]Rorty, *The Consequences of Pragmatism*, p. xliii.

[10]Jean-Paul Sartre, *Existentialism* (New York: Philosophical Library, 1947), pp. 36-37.

[11]Rorty, *The Consequences of Pragmatism*, p. xlii.

[12]Rorty, *Contingency, Irony and Solidarity*, p. 67.

[13]Ibid., p. 9.

[14]Charles Taylor points up the dilemma facing Rorty *(Reading Rorty*, pp. 257-75), as does Bernard Williams, "Auto-da-Fé: Consequences of Pragmatism," in *Reading Rorty*, pp. 26-37.

[15]Campbell and Moyers, *The Power of Myth*, p. 21.

[16]James W. Sire, *The Discipleship of the Mind* (Downers Grove, Ill.: InterVarsity Press, 1990), chaps. 5-6, pp. 79-113.

Chapter 7: Three's a Company

[1]The book Chris's sociology professor had recommended, Robert Bellah et al., *Habits*

of the Heart (New York: Harper & Row, 1985), is an excellent illustration of how a Christian sociologist, along with his colleagues, can do sociology. Although their work is a major contribution to human knowledge in general, it also represents a distinctive contribution from a Christian perspective.

Chapter 8: One's Enough

[1]William Ernest Henley (1849-1903), "Invictus."

[2]Robert Bellah et al., *Habits of the Heart* (New York: Harper & Row, 1985), p. 143.

[3]Hans Jonas, *The Imperative of Responsibility* (Chicago: University of Chicago Press, 1984), p. 84.

[4]Bellah et al., *Habits,* p. 33.

[5]Ibid., p. 336.

[6]Ibid., p. 35.

[7]Ibid., p. 34.

[8]Joseph Campbell with Michael Toms, *An Open Life* (New York: Harper & Row, 1989), p. 90.

[9]I have analyzed the New Age movement in more detail in *The Universe Next Door,* 2nd ed. (Downers Grove, Ill.: InterVarsity Press, 1988), pp. 156-208; and *Shirley MacLaine and the New Age Movement* (Downers Grove, Ill.: InterVarsity Press, 1988).

[10]Shirley MacLaine, *It's All in the Playing* (New York: Bantam, 1987), p. 174.

[11]Anthony Ugolnik, *The Illuminating Icon* (Grand Rapids, Mich.: Eerdmans, 1989), pp. 99-100).

[12]Ibid., p. 100.

[13]Ibid., p. 164.

[14]Quoted by Roland H. Bainton, *The Reformation of the Sixteenth Century* (Boston: Beacon, 1952), p. 61.

[15]Ibid.

[16]Czeslaw Milosz, *Visions of San Francisco Bay,* trans. Richard Lourie (New York: Farrar Straus Giroux, 1982), pp. 42-43.

[17]Glenn Tinder, "Can We Be Good Without God?" *The Atlantic,* December 1989, p. 72; see also his *The Political Meaning of Christianity: An Interpretation* (Baton Rouge: Louisiana State University Press, 1989).

[18]Ibid.

[19]Jacob Weisberg, "Thin Skins," *The New Republic,* February 18, 1991, p. 22.

[20]"The Derisory Tower," *The New Republic,* February 18, 1991, p. 5.

[21]Ibid.

[22]Theodore Roszak, *Where the Wasteland Ends* (New York: Doubleday, 1973), p. 449, quoted in Os Guinness, *The Gravedigger File* (Downers Grove, Ill.: InterVarsity Press, 1983), p. 79.

Chapter 9: Four's a Community

[1]For a source for the story of Chuang Chou (who lived between 399 and 295 B.C.), see *A Source Book in Chinese Philosophy,* trans. Wing-tsit Chan (Princeton, N.J.: Princeton University Press, 1963), p. 190.

[2]Lesslie Newbigin, *The Gospel in a Pluralist Society* (Grand Rapids, Mich.: Eerdmans, 1989), pp. 8, 21, 47-48.

Chapter 10: Community amid Chaos
[1]Walther Eichrodt, *The Theology of the Old Testament* (London: SCM, 1967), 2:265, as quoted in Bruce Milne, *We Belong Together* (Downers Grove, Ill.: InterVarsity Press, 1978), p. 18.
[2]Quoted by Dietrich Bonhoeffer, *Life Together*, trans. John W. Doberstein (London: SCM, 1954), pp. 7-8.
[3]Bonhoeffer, *Life Together*, pp. 17-18.
[4]Ibid., p. 16.
[5]Ibid., p. 29.

Chapter 11: Bob Wong's Search for Jesus
[1]Many Bible study guides are useful for investigative Bible studies. I especially recommend those that focus on one of the Gospels or material from several of them. My own *Meeting Jesus* (Wheaton, Ill.: Harold Shaw, 1988) is explicitly designed for a situation like that faced by Chris and Bill. Others can be selected from InterVarsity Press's series of LifeGuide Bible Studies or the Fisherman Bible Studies published by Harold Shaw.

For general help in leading Bible studies see Ada Lum, *How to Begin an Evangelistic Bible Study* (Downers Grove, Ill.: InterVarsity Press, 1971); James F. Nyquist, *Leading Bible Discussions*, 2nd ed. (Downers Grove, Ill.: InterVarsity Press, 1985); and Peter Scazzero, *Introducing Jesus* (Downers Grove, Ill.: InterVarsity Press, 1991).

The form of apologetic argument that this chapter illustrates is the liar-lunatic-Lord trilemma made famous by C. S. Lewis in *Mere Christianity* (New York: Macmillan, 1981), pp. 55-56. Other developments of this argument, very useful to people wanting to polish their skills in dialogue with non-Christian friends, include Peter Kreeft, *Between Heaven and Hell* (Downers Grove, Ill.: InterVarsity Press, 1982), and Josh McDowell, *More than a Carpenter* (Wheaton, Ill.: Tyndale House, 1980).

Chapter 13: The Public Face of Christianity
[1]James Davison Hunter and Os Guinness, *Articles of Faith, Articles of Peace* (Washington, D.C.: Brookings Institution, 1990); and *The Journal of Law and Religion* 8, no. 1-2 (1990). Both contain the text of and commentary on the Williamsburg Charter. Evangelicals for Social Action (10 Lancaster Ave., Wynnewood, PA 19096) publishes a newsletter, as does the Center for Public Justice (806 Fifteenth St. NW, Suite 440, Washington, DC 20005). Trinity Forum can contacted at 9587 Bronte Drive, Burke, VA 22015.
[2]For much of this discussion of privatization and the diagram (figure 1) I am indebted to my colleagues on InterVarsity staff, especially James Paternoster.
[3]Os Guinness, *The Gravedigger File* (Downers Grove, Ill.: InterVarsity Press, 1983), p. 74.
[4]See the profile and interview of C. Everett Koop by Philip Yancey, "The Embattled Career of Dr. Koop," *Christianity Today*, October 20, 1989, pp. 30-34; and "Surgeon

General's Warning: An Interview with C. Everett Koop," *Christianity Today*, November 3, 1989), pp. 16-19.

[5]I am indebted to Richard Mouw, *When the Kings Come Marching In* (Grand Rapids, Mich.: Eerdmans, 1983), for much of what follows here.

[6]Ibid., pp. 25-26.

[7]Ibid., p. 37.

[8]Ibid., pp. 38-39.

[9]John Howard Yoder, *The Politics of Jesus* (Grand Rapids, Mich.: Eerdmans, 1972), pp. 97.

[10]Guinness, *The Gravedigger File*, pp. 79-80.

[11]Lesslie Newbigin, *Foolishness to the Greeks* (Grand Rapids, Mich.: Eerdmans, 1986), p. 124.

Chapter 14: The Thinker Prays

[1]John has begun to realize a bit of what Tatiana Goricheva experienced. Goricheva, a brilliant philosophy student in St. Petersburg (formerly Leningrad), recounts her trek from Marxist-Leninist ideology on into existentialism, nihilism and then yoga. While yoga provided a breakthrough into an understanding that there was a spiritual realm, it did not satisfy. "But in a yoga book a Christian prayer, the 'Our Father', was suggested as an exercise. . . . I began to say it as a mantra, automatically and without expression. I said it about six times, and then I was suddenly turned inside out. I understood—not with my ridiculous understanding, but with my whole being—that he exists. He, the living personal God who lives in me and all creatures, who has created the world, who became a human being out of love, the crucified and risen God. At that moment I understood and grasped the 'mystery' of Christianity, the new, true life. That was real, genuine deliverance. At this moment everything in me changed. The old me died. I gave up not only my earlier values and ideals, but also my old habits" (Tatiana Goricheva, *Talking About God Is Dangerous: The Diary of a Russian Dissident*, trans. John Bowden [New York: Crossroads, 1986], pp. 17-18).